SEARCHIN
TOGETH

Originally founded in 1972 as the _,
Reformation Review, *Searching Together* is
a journal published quarterly by Quoir.
Thanks primarily to the work of Jon and
Dotty Zens—and the support of various
volunteers and groups over the years—
this publication has sought to stir up
the body of Christ, challenge thought,
create dialogue, encourage, and build up
the followers of Christ far and wide.

Since 1982, *Searching Together* has carried on with the founding thought of the
first editor, Norbert Ward: "[We] make no
claim to be the voice of a movement or an
organized denomination. We do not, on
the other hand, claim to be a lone voice.
We believe that we are expressing the hope
and earnest prayer of concerned believers."

Over the years, *Searching Together* has
focused on the themes of the life of Christ
in His body, getting along with one
another, and the implications of being
the Bride of Christ in a fallen culture. We
long to be saturated with the cry of Paul's
heart—"the love of Christ compels me..."
Herman Ridderbos emphasized that the
Gospel finds its most central and fundamental expression in love. "In the first
place, this love derives its central significance from the fact that it is the reflection
of the love of God in Jesus Christ. The
love of God revealed in Christ's self-sur-
render and working itself out by the
Holy Spirit in the love of the church is
the real secret and clearest expression of
its holiness."

We trust that this issue of *Searching
Together* will encourage you in the love
of Christ.

JON ZENS

ST TEAM
JAMES BERLING
BOBBYE BOWER
SHAMRA & DALE MARTIN
RAFAEL & TEIGHLOR POLENDO
ARLAN PURDY
JODI & MARV ROOT
HEATHER TOFTNESS
CHARLENE WILDER
MARY ELLEN ROBINSON
GRAHAM WOOD
ROGER PESUIT

PUBLISHER
QUOIR
ORANGE, CA
QUOIR.COM

**COVER DESIGN &
INTERIOR LAYOUT**
RAFAEL POLENDO
POLENDO.NET

COVER IMAGE
TRANSFIGURATION OF CHRIST
BY CARL HEINRICH BLOCH
1872
PUBLIC DOMAIN

ISBN
978-1-938480-34-8

**VOLUME 44:03-04
FALL-WINTER 2018**

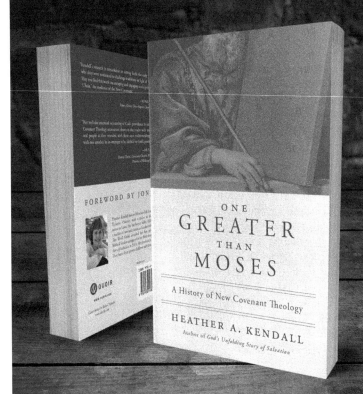

CONTENTS

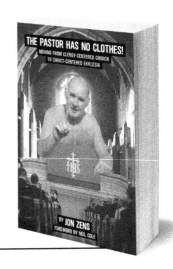

THE GOSPEL AND THE LAW OF CHRIST

C.H. DODD (1884-1973)

This 1946 Lecture by C.H. Dodd could very well be marked as a significant turning point in New Testament theology. The truth is, since Dodd's presentation numerous New Testament scholars of all stripes have come to recognize that the Christian ethic is rooted in the historical Christ-event. Just as Israel's covenant life was based on God's action in the Red Sea exodus, so the Church's new covenant life flows out the new exodus at Golgotha. As Douglas Webster notes, "The Christian ethic is exclusively dependent upon Christian redemption…Jesus' cross is planted squarely at the center of the believer's existence, providing both the means of salvation and the challenge of a new life-style" (A Passion for Christ: Toward An Evangelical Christology, *Zondervan, 1987, pp. 149,153). —Jon Zens*

The Christian religion has its centre in the Gospel, which is defined as "the Gospel of the glory of the blessed God" (1 Tim. 1:11); or (which comes to the same thing) "the Gospel of the glory of Christ, who is the image of God" (2 Cor. 4:4).

This Gospel was embodied in the apostolic *kerygma*, or "proclamation," with which the first witnesses to Christianity went out into the world. The *kerygma* is built up about a story of events which had recently happened: how Jesus of Nazareth, anointed with the Holy Spirit, went about doing good and healing all who were oppressed by the devil; how He went up with His followers from Galilee to Jerusalem, was betrayed, condemned, crucified and buried; on the third day He rose from the dead; He was exalted to the right hand of God; from thence He rules His people through His Spirit, until at the end He shall be revealed as Judge and Saviour of men. These events are set forth as the fulfilment of God's purpose declared by ancient prophecy. In them His Kingdom has come upon men.

Such, in barest outline, is the pattern of the apostolic "proclamation," as we can reconstruct it from a comparison of various passages of the New Testament. It was in such terms that the Gospel was proclaimed from the first days of Christianity. It is essentially a story—a history of things that happened, with the meaning that they bore; for no story rises to the full dignity of history unless in recording occurrences it discloses something of their meaning. We need not apologize for the Gospel story in such terms as those of Tennyson's patronizing lines—

"Truth embodied in a tale
Shall enter in at lowly doors."
The Gospel of the glory of God is properly set forth in a story of action, because the glory of God is revealed in His "mighty acts. This is an assumption that runs all through the Bible. For the comparative study of religion it characterizes primitive Christianity over against the highest kind of religion which it encountered in the Graeco-Roman world. This kind of religion, derived partly from Greek rationalism and partly from oriental mysticism, offered the vision of God as pure Being, immobile, unchanging, undifferentiated, definable ultimately only by negatives. It is of more than merely historical interest, because it is a type of religion tenacious of life and influence down to our own time, and is often confused with Christianity. In contrast, the prophetic religion of Israel proclaimed the glory of God by telling how He brought up His people out of Egypt, gave them an inheritance in Canaan, raised up David to be their king, chastised their unfaithfulness by the rod of Assyria and Babylon, restored them from exile, and bade them wait and hope for the coming of His Kingdom in the fullness of time. Primitive Christianity repeated this story, and added the missing climax:—"The time is fulfilled, and the Kingdom of God is at hand"; "God has visited and redeemed His people."

In this story of His mighty acts, the glory of God is revealed, but most especially in the events which form its climax—in the life, death and resurrection of Jesus Christ. Here we may recognize most clearly the *direction* which divine action takes—or, if you will, the purpose at which it aims—and the quality of the action itself. To put it briefly, the divine action is directed towards the restoration of wholeness (*redintegratio*) to His living creation, at large and in each individual part of it. The quality of the divine action is denominated in the New Testament by the untranslatable word *agapé*: the love of God, we must translate it, or the divine charity, remembering always that *agapé* is not warm feeling, but an energy of goodwill, inexhaustible, unlimited by the worthiness or unworthiness of its objects, and going to the utmost lengths of self-sacrifice on their behalf. To men whose lives are spoiled and enslaved by sin, the divine *agapé* is known as power to forgive, heal and renew. Hence the Gospel of the glory of God comes to us as a Gospel of salvation.

The essential thing here is that the Gospel tells us what God has done for us, not—except by inference or implication—what we should do. Its most succinct and impressive expression is the well-known verse, John 3:16. This classical statement acquaints us first with God's attitude to the world (He loved it); then with the action in which that attitude found expression (He gave His Son); and finally with the purpose which directed that action, and its consequences for mankind (the attainment of eternal life). With all this in view, the same evangelist reports: "We beheld His glory."

The renewed emphasis upon the Gospel as a proclamation of what God has done is a feature of Christian thought in our own time which marks a real change of religious climate. In this country at least the idea has often prevailed that religion is "morality touched with emotion," and Christianity a lofty code of ethics, enlivened by sentiments of reverence towards God and towards Christ as the revealer of His will. As such, it was commended as a valuable aid to the ethical improvement of human society. The underlying assumption was that of the child who when told to pray, "God make me a good girl," replied, "I wouldn't trouble God about a little thing like that: I can be good by myself if I want to." This is in fact the theology of Pelagius, the first British theologian known to history. The atmosphere in which many of us grew up had a good deal of native Pelagianism in it, as indeed our Continental brethren have not been slow to point out. Recent events, however, have thrown doubt upon the cheerful optimism about human nature which Pelagianism implies. When we contemplate the condition of the world—its moral condition, in which we are all implicated—we are driven to say, with shuddering conviction, "It is of Thy mercies that we are not consumed." We realize now, if we did not before, that Christian preaching, if it is to meet the need of us all, must be something more than variations on the theme, "Be good." We begin to understand why Paul said that it pleased God to save men by the foolishness of the *kerygma*, the word preached, and not by instruction in morals, however wise.

It is a salutary change which has brought Christian thought back to this point. And yet—Christianity *is* an ethical religion. Is it necessary to say this with any emphasis? Perhaps not; though there is a not uninfluential school which shows some uneasiness at any emphatic insistence upon the "social-ethical" implications of Christianity, as though it detracted from the pure Gospel of the glory of God. Christianity, they tell us, must at all costs not be made into a new law. Did not the Apostle write, "Christ is the end of the law to every one that believeth" (Romans 10:4)? True enough; yet Paul himself called upon his converts to "fulfil the law of Christ" (Galatians 6:2). If we owe to him that fundamental affirmation, "By grace were ye saved, through faith, and that not of yourselves, it is the gift of God; not of works, lest any man should boast" (Ephesians 2:8), we must also attend to him when he says: "Work out your own salvation with fear and trembling" (Philippians 2:12). Once indeed he gives us a momentary glimpse of the intensity of his own struggle to fulfil the law of Christ: "My fight is no shadow-boxing: I bruise my body and make it know its master, lest having preached to others I should myself become a cast-away" (1 Corinthians 9:26-27). That last clause must strike deep into the conscience of every preacher of the Gospel. But indeed the importance of conduct is written into the very structure of the New Testament. The Gospels, as one of their authors observes, are about "all that Jesus began *both* to do *and* to teach" (Acts 1:1), and the regular pattern of the epistles falls into two balanced parts: a "theological" part, which is an exposition of the Gospel, and an "ethical" part, which lays down the lines of Christian conduct. We may perhaps clinch the matter briefly by citing one of the less-remembered beatitudes of our Lord: "Blessed are they that hear the word of God, and keep it" (Luke 11:28).

It is not really necessary to prove that Christianity contains *both* a Gospel about what God has done, *and also* directions about what man should do. But I want to ask, how the Law of Christ is related to the Gospel of Christ, and what light this relation throws upon the nature and the range of Christian obligation.

First, then, God's revelation of Himself to men is represented in the Bible—both in the Old Testament and in the New—in the form of a *covenant* between God and man. A covenant is what they call a "bilateral agreement." It is true that between the Creator and His creatures there can be no question of a negotiated agreement on equal terms. The initiative lies entirely with God, and He alone defines the terms of agreement, by His sovereign will. Yet the acceptance of the covenant by the other party, man, is an equally essential part of the transaction. Thus man is not a passive recipient but an active party to the covenant, however sub-ordinate his action may be to the divine action by which the whole is initiated and validated.

There is here something thoroughly characteristic of the biblical conception of God. I have already referred to that high type of religion prevalent in the world to which Christianity first came, and by no means obsolete today, which offered to initiate men into the vision of God as absolute Being. In such a revelation man's part is to stand back and contemplate the divine perfection. He need not *do* anything about it. No *active* relation between God and man is involved. Indeed, many of these thinkers would have held that any such active relation, if it were possible, would disturb our apprehension of the Absolute, since it would introduce an element of movement or change. In the biblical view, on the other hand, the glory of God is revealed in action upon the changing field of history, and the way of receiving such revelation is responsive action on the part of man, and not mere contemplation.

Thus the pattern of the covenant, in both Testaments, consists, on the one hand, of a declaration of the divine action through which the covenant was initiated, and, on the other hand, of the corresponding obligation which man undertakes. The Old Covenant runs thus: "I am the Lord thy God, which brought thee up out of the land of Egypt"— and then—"Thou shalt have none other gods before me...

Remember the Sabbath Day…Honour father and mother… Thou shalt not kill …" God took action to initiate the covenant by working the deliverance of Israel out of Egyptian slavery, and Israel responded by undertaking these, and the like, defined obligations. In that reciprocal action the self-revelation of God became an operative fact in history. In the New Testament the scene of the inauguration of the New Covenant is the Last Supper of Jesus with His disciples. In the Pauline and Synoptic accounts of the Supper it is said to be inaugurated "in His blood." That is to say, the whole career of Jesus, as the Servant who "came not to be ministered unto but to minister, and to give His life a ransom for many," is the divine action by which the covenant is initiated. The corresponding obligation is not explicitly stated in the Synoptic and Pauline accounts of the Supper, but in the Fourth Gospel we read how on the same occasion Jesus gave ocular demonstration of His role of Servant by washing His disciples' feet, and thereupon solemnly added, "I have set you an example, that you should do as I have done to you… A New Commandment I give you, that you should love one another; as I have loved you, you are to love one another" (John 13: 15, 34). Such is the obligation entailed by the New Covenant "in the blood of Christ."

This Johannine form of statement is highly significant. We have already seen that the most succinct and comprehensive statement of the Gospel, as a proclamation of what God has done for us, is the famous verse beginning, "God so loved the world." We now learn, from the same Evangelist, that the required response, by which the covenant takes effect, is an imitation, or reproduction in our own lives, of the divine charity which found active expression in the work of Christ.

That which is the central purport of the Gospel is at the same time the content of the Law of Christ.

This intimate relation, or even identity, between the Gospel and the Law of Christ is most forcibly expressed in the First Epistle of John. The thought of this short writing all moves about the idea of "the word of life," which indeed the author declares at the beginning to be his main theme. The word of life—that utterance of the Eternal which conveys life to His creatures—is at once Gospel and Commandment. On the one hand, "The love of God was disclosed in this: that He sent His Son into the world that we might live through Him…in this, not that we loved God but that He loved us and sent His Son to expiate our sins" (1 John 4:9-10)—a statement of the Gospel which may be placed alongside the classical passage, John 3:16. On the other side, "If God so loved us, we ought also to love one another" (1 John 4:11). So far the two run side by side. But it is the fusion of these two aspects of the "word of life" into a single statement that is so significant: "God is love: He who dwells in love dwells in God and God dwells in him"; and again, "We love, because He first loved us" (1 John 4:16, 19). In such maxims the divine charity which is the theme of the Gospel, and the charity towards men which is the "new commandment" of the Law of Christ, are inseparable. It should be added that this author has left us no excuse for supposing that *agapé* can be anything other than action. There is a downright con-creteness, almost crudity, in his test for the presence of *agapé* in human relations: "If any possesses the means of earthly existence, and sees his brother and shuts his heart against him, how can the divine charity dwell in him?" (1 John 3:17). This last passage will suggest further reflections presently. But let us at this point report progress so far. We have learnt that Gospel and Commandment are two sides, or aspects, of a single reality, or rather activity, which is *agapé*, the love of God, the divine charity; and *agapé* in action is the glory of God revealed, whether it be His own redemptive act in Christ, or the simplest act of charity which His lowliest creature is enabled by His grace to perform; since of any such act it must be said "We love, because He first loved us."

The passage which I quoted from 1 John 3: 17 may serve as a warning which seems to be needed at this stage of our enquiry. When we are seeking the fundamental relation of Law and Gospel in Christianity, we are driven to this central point at which the single principle of *agapé* is seen to be variously embodied in both. But we should be far from a full appreciation of the nature of the Law of Christ if we left the matter at this rather rarefied and abstract level. Augustine's "Love and do as you like" has the value of a challenging epigram, but it can be seriously misleading. It is too much exposed to the danger of a barren sentimentality. At any rate few of the New Testament writers seem to have been content to leave it at that. Most of them spend a good deal of their paper upon quite specific injunctions for Christian conduct in a variety of actual situations. Most notably of all, the teaching of our Lord, as it is given in the Synoptic Gospels, is full of concrete and particularized precepts. Indeed, it is only when He was challenged directly to define the "first and greatest commandment" that He allowed Himself so broad a generalization as, "Thou shalt love the Lord thy God with all thy heart, and thy neighbour as thyself." For the most part He deals with concrete situations, and His precepts are even embarrassingly particular. "If anyone strikes you on one cheek, turn the other cheek." "If you are offering your gift at the altar, and it suddenly comes to your mind that your brother has something against you, leave your gift there before the altar; go and make it up with your brother, and then come back and go on with your offering." "When you are giving a luncheon or dinner party, do not invite your friends and relations and your rich neighbours in case they should invite you back… Invite people who are poor, crippled, lame and blind."

I need not quote further. It is notoriously difficult to take such precepts literally and at the same time to apply them as practicable rules for daily life. In attempting to expound the ethical teaching of Jesus we are often driven to such terms as "paradox" and "hyperbole." But if we take such terms to denote nothing more than figures of speech or rhetorical devices to give emphasis or to stimulate reflection, we are not going deep enough. Jesus certainly intended His precepts to be taken seriously.

We must however enquire exactly what they were intended to convey. It is in fact clear that very few of them are of such a kind that they could be adopted without alteration or expansion into a code of regulations enforceable, if necessary, by competent legal authority. They contrast sharply in this respect with much contemporary Jewish teaching, which was designed by the Rabbis expressly to lay down legally enforceable rules of discipline. The sayings of Jesus must have had some different intention.

At this point we may go back to the idea of the Covenant upon which our obligation to the Law of Christ is grounded. At an earlier point in this lecture we noted the *similarity* between the old and new covenants. The pattern of both is identical: a recital of the "mighty acts of God," and a statement of His demands. Now we must note a *difference*. In Jeremiah 31: 31 *seqq.*, the prophet describes the New Covenant in these terms: "I will put my law in their inward parts, and in their heart will I write it." That passage is quoted at length in Hebrews 8: 8-12 as the programme, so to speak, of the work of Christ. Paul echoes its language in the chapter (2 Corinthians 3) where he contrasts the old covenant and the new. He speaks of an "epistle of Christ, written not upon tables of stone, but upon fleshly tables of the heart, not with ink, but with the Spirit of the living God." Accordingly, while the old law was an "administration of the written word (*gramma*)," the New Covenant is an "administration of the Spirit."

What precisely is the difference intended? The description of the Law of Moses as *gramma*, a written document, is tolerably clear (though Paul has pardonably confused an inscription on stone with a document written in ink!). Each commandment, he means, is set down in black and white, ready to be transferred directly to the field of daily conduct. It is, as Paul describes it elsewhere, a "law of commandments contained in ordinances." As such, he insists, it is abolished by Christ. But what exactly is meant by a law written on the heart, a law of the Spirit? It is inward, in some sense, while the other is external. But that is not to say that there is no law for the Christian but that of his own "inner light." "To every man his own conscience is God." That sentiment, I believe, would meet with widespread applause, under the impression that it was Christian; but it is the sentiment of a pagan poet (Menander), and it is at variance with the Christian belief in a Law of God which is above the conscience. It is indeed difficult to maintain, in face of the New Testament, the once popular view that Christianity is a "religion of the Spirit" in contrast to "religions of authority." It is observed of our Lord in the Gospels that "He taught them as one having authority," and He Himself affirmed the authority of His own words in the parable of the two builders: "Everyone who hears these sayings of mine and does not put them into practice shall be compared to a foolish man who built his house upon the sand"—with disastrous results which I need not repeat. The difference between "the administration of the written word" and "the administration of the Spirit" is not precisely that between objective and subjective moral standards.

Let us then look again at the precepts of Jesus as they are given in the Gospels. They are not—so much we may now take for granted—a "law of commandments contained in ordinances," but a law, in some sense, written on the heart, by the Spirit.

Fundamentally, as we have seen, the Law of Christ may be stated in the form of His own New Commandment—"Love one another, as I have loved you." In other words, Christian morality consists in giving effect, within human relations, to the divine charity which is the glory of God, disclosed in the work of Christ. The several precepts, therefore, may be regarded as examples of the way in which divine charity may become effective in various relations and situations occurring in the course of our lives. The standard of reference is always the love of God. In some sayings this is made quite explicit. "Be merciful as your Father is merciful." "Love your enemies, that you may be sons of your Father in heaven." Consequently there is an absoluteness, an infinitude, about the obligations of the Law of Christ, which makes it impossible to state them in terms of precision directly applicable to workaday conditions. But what *is* possible is to give clear-cut pictures of the way in which divine charity would work in certain definite human situations, supposing it to work freely, unhindered by, the obstacles which are interposed both by our own weakness, obtuseness and depravity, and by the pressure of a sinful order of society.

If we take the precepts of Jesus in this way, they serve to keep us in mind of a standard or ideal of conduct which lies always far beyond our attainment. It is no wonder they impress us with a sense of paradox or hyperbole. If we supposed for a moment that we could ever love our enemies, or even our friendly neighbours, as God loved us in Christ, we should only show how far we were from understanding the "Gospel of the glory of the blessed God"; and yet that very Gospel makes such love obligatory upon us. Christ's law clearly demands our full obedience, and yet—"When you have done all, say, 'We are unprofitable servants; we have only done our duty'"—and how many of us could say as much as that? The precepts of Christ therefore are our judge; and in judging us, they expose our desperate need for forgiveness, and throw us back again and again upon the inexhaustible mercies of God. Thus the Law of Christ serves to make us more keenly aware of the depths of the Gospel.

But that is not all. Jesus did expect of His followers that they should obey His precepts, even though He recognized that their obedience would never bring them to absolute fulfilment of the demands of God, just because God's demands are in their nature as infinite as is His own love. His precepts indicate, in vivid pictures, the *quality*, and the *direction*, of any action which is to conform to the love of God. This quality may be present, in its degree, at quite a lowly level of performance, and the right direction may be clearly discernible in the act even though the goal is still far off.

Take for example the injunction to "turn the other cheek." It is hardly possible to treat that as a ruling to be directly applied in all appropriate circumstances. It is not only that we may not be good enough to put it into practice. It may not, in the confused and distorted state of human affairs, be always the best thing to do. On the other hand, it can hardly be regarded as the ideal for conduct in an ideally perfect society. In such a society the contingency would not arise. But the picture which Jesus draws sets before us vividly, in the context of an imperfect society, the patience, the detachment from egoism and pride, and the respect for other people, even the most objectionable, which we can clearly see to conform to God's action towards us in Christ. We are to imitate, in our measure, His forbearance under affronts, His respect for our freedom which will not allow Him to coerce, and His endless patience. And these qualities must give character to Christian action even at a lowly level; even if all we can manage is a half-frustrated effort to overcome, or at least to moderate, our natural pride, resentment and impatience for Christ's sake. In making that effort, if it is honestly made, we have obeyed the command of Christ, since the very effort has in it the quality, and moves in the direction, which He prescribes; while every such effort will help us to realize afresh the immense distance that still separates us from perfect fulfilment of His Law. The characteristic response of one who had gone a very long way on the road is this: "I count not myself to have apprehended, neither to be already made perfect; but one thing I do: forgetting that which is behind and reaching out to that which is before, I press towards the mark for the prize of the high calling of God in Christ Jesus" (Philippians 3:13-14).

If in this spirit we keep the commands of Christ steadily before us, reflecting upon them, yet treating them not merely as objects for contemplation but as spurs to action, there is built up in us a certain outlook upon life, a bias of mind, a standard of moral judgment. The Law of Christ, in fact, is "written on our hearts." His precepts cannot be directly trans- ferred from the written page to action. They must become, through reflection and through effort, increasingly a part of our total outlook upon life, of the total bias of our minds. Then they will find expression in action appropriate to the changing situations in which we find ourselves.

This point, that the precepts of Christ are not statutory definitions like those of the Mosaic Code, but indications of *quality* and *direction* of action, which may be present at quite lowly levels of performance, is very important when we con- sider the application of Christian moral standards to human society at large. The Church claims, and rightly claims, to pronounce moral judgments upon human conduct in social and international relations, far beyond the limits of its own membership. It does so, not in the sense that it supposes the highest Christian ideals to be directly practicable in these spheres, but in the sense that unless human action, even in these spheres, has the quality and the direction demanded by the Law of Christ, it is wrong and stands condemned. It may be neither possible nor desirable for nations to act like the man who turns the other cheek, but even at such a moment as this in the affairs of the world, human action is wrong, unless it partakes of this quality, of a patient and unself-re- garding respect for the other party, however objectionable;

and aims in this direction, towards "overcoming evil with good." Unless it does so, it is not only wrong, but ultimately disastrous.

For the Law of Christ is not a specialized code of regulations for a society with optional membership. It is based upon a revelation of the nature of the eternal God, and it affirms the principles upon which His world is built, and which men ignore at their peril. It is noteworthy that in setting forth His teaching our Lord more than once appeals to the established order of creation as a pointer to the Law of God. One remarkable instance is His legislation about divorce. The Law of Moses, He says, permitted divorce; but this was only a concession to human obtuseness. "From the beginning of creation 'male and female created He them…and the twain shall be one flesh.'" Hence follows the conclusion: "Whom God hath joined together, let no man put asunder" (Mark 10:6-9). That is to say, in spite of the law of Moses, the very nature of man, as created by God, points, if properly understood, to the law of permanent monogamy. Again, when He is laying down what has often been regarded as the most distinctive, even the most paradoxical, element in the Christian law, He argues from the order of created nature: "Love your enemies, that you may be sons of your Father in heaven, for He makes the sun shine on evil and good, and rains on just and unjust" (Matthew 5:44-45). Again, it is presupposed in many of His sayings and parables that there are human relationships on the natural level-such as those of parent and child, king and subject, master and servant, friend and friend—which disclose, upon examination, certain principles or maxims which are the mirror of the Creator's pattern for human life. In maxims we may already discern something of the quality and direction which human action must have if it is to conform with the ultimate law of divine charity. "If ye, being evil, know how to give good gifts to your children, how much more your Father in heaven." Parental care for children is a part of man's natural endowment. It falls far short of the perfect fatherhood of God, but it has the same quality, and moves in the same direction, as the love of God Himself. Conversely, we are justified in saying, if a parent does not give his children as good gifts as he can manage, there is a breach of the Law of God; and the parent is subject to this judgment, whether he is a Christian or not, because the Law of God, which is revealed and interpreted in Christ, is a universal law, capable of being observed in its measure at every level, while infinite in its ultimate range.

The conscience of man, it appears, is a kind of palimpsest—like one of those ancient parchments which many of our libraries possess, from which the original script had been erased long ago, in order that the expensive material might be used by another writer. It is often possible by careful scrutiny to decipher here and there a word of the underlying script. So we may think of the Law of God as having been "written on the heart" of man by the mere fact of his creation: in fact Paul says as much in Romans 2:14-15. But by reason of the perversity of the human will, the depravity of human society, and all that is comprehended in the ideas of the fall of man and original sin, the writing is hard to decipher. Where however something of it may be dimly read, it can be recognized as a first draft of that revelation of the will of God which is given to us clear and fresh in Christ.

Something like this seems to be implied in the Prologue to the Fourth Gospel. We read there about the Word of God, by which all things were made. This Word is the light that enlightens every man who comes into the world, without exception. Yet the world does not know it. At last the Word was made flesh and dwelt among us, and we beheld His glory—the same Word by which the worlds were made and man was fashioned, and his mind made capable of truth.

The Word of life is Gospel and Law at once, and in both the glory of the Lord is revealed, that all flesh may see it together. The Gospel which tells us what God has done, and the Law which tells us what He commands, are both to be understood through the historic personality, the words and the actions, of Jesus Christ, the Word made flesh. ■

A special thanks and hat's off to Graham Wood (York, UK) for his effort in taking articles from the past and turning them into Word documents for this project. You are amazing, Graham!

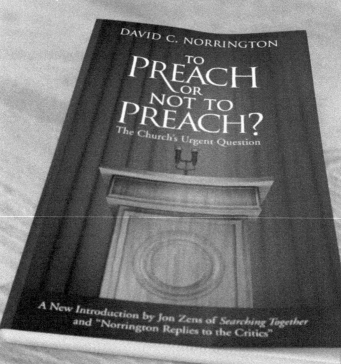

A LITTLE BACKGROUND

JON ZENS

While at Westminster Seminary in 1972 I wrote a paper on Jonathan Edwards. I had heard that E.W. Johnson in Pine Bluff, Arkansas, was an Edwards buff, so I sent him a copy. He read it, and forwarded it to Norbert Ward who had started publishing *Baptist Reformation Review* in 1972. Norbert ended up putting my article in the Fall, 1973, *BRR*.

Norbert had lived in Cincinnati, Ohio, area for many years and was the audio coordinator for a Landmark Baptist radio preacher, Lasserre Bradley, Jr., whose program began in 1953. Around 1969 Norbert moved to Nashville, Tennessee, to be a sound engineer for CBS Records.

In Nashville he attended a Landmark Baptist Church. However, Norbert began listening to the messages of Rolfe Barnard, Henry Mahan in Ashland, Kentucky, E.W. Johnson in Arkansas and others. His heart was enlarged to see the free grace of God in Christ more clearly. As a result of this revelation, he began to have serious questions about key Landmark doctrines. When he shared his concerns with the Nashville leadership, he was ultimately excommunicated.

Prior to his excommunication, Norbert started a mimeographed broadsheet, *Inquire*, which tackled various in-house Baptist issues with multiple viewpoints expressed in a dialogical manner. After his removal from Landmark circles, he wondered what to do with his publishing desires. His new preacher friends in the South encouraged him to continue writing, so in 1972 the quarterly *Baptist Reformation Review* was launched.

In Volume 1, Number 1, founding editor Norbert Ward stated his foundational perspectives.

> "[We] make no claim to be the voice of a movement or an organized denomination. We do not, on the other hand, claim to be a lone voice. We believe that we are expressing the hope and earnest prayer of concerned believers…I also have a theory of my own about systematic theology: a theologian who is completely systematic with himself has probably rejected at least 50% of Biblical truth."

Around 1974 Norbert, using his gifts in the recording industry, compiled, edited and enhanced a number of messages by Rolfe Barnard (1904-1969), and produced a multiple-record LP vinyl set. His effort was a real encouragement to many in the mid-1970's.

In the summer of 1974, we met Norbert at the Reformed

Baptist Family Conference in Harvey Cedars, New Jersey. In the course of our conversations together, he invited us to move to Nashville. We moved to Nashville in 1975 to be part of the fellowship that met in his home, and to work with Norbert on the magazine.

In late 1977, Norbert experienced some serious health challenges. As a result of these set-backs, in early 1978 he asked then Associate Editor Jon Zens, who had moved to Nashville in 1975, to become Editor of *BRR*. On September 14, 1980, Norbert passed to be with His Lord. Fittingly, Henry Mahan beautifully preached Jesus Christ at his funeral service.

Norbert was a brother given a rare combination of love and wisdom, and a strong desire to see Christ lifted up in his generation. I certainly count it as a privilege and an honor to have fellowshipped and worked with him. ∎

On August 31, 2017, Chris Fales interviewed Jon Zens concerning his journey to Christ as our New Covenant, 1972–2017. Fall 2017 marked the 40th anniversary of Jon's ground-breaking article, "Is There A 'Covenant of Grace'?" In 1980, John Reisinger called this article "the first shot fired in 20 years!" Here are the links to the interview and the 1977 article.

http://biblethumpingwingnut.com/2017/09/02/cftp-episode-62-words-interview-jon-zens/

http://www.searchingtogether.org/articles/covenant.htm

LAW AND MINISTRY IN THE CHURCH: AN INFORMAL ESSAY ON SOME PATHWAYS OF MY JOURNEY (1972–1984)

JON ZENS, 1984 (REVISED MAY 2012)

In early 1984, Drew Garner of Houston, Texas, called and asked if I would write a paper about my pilgrimage toward Christ in the New Covenant. He needed this to use in his research for an historical paper he was presenting at a pastor's conference. This is it.

In the past few years requests have appeared for "background" history regarding some of the issues dealt with in *Searching Together* (formerly *Baptist Reformation Review* [*BRR*]). This essay will overview some historical highlights based on the author's experiences. The historical events will be considered with reference to two issues: the law/gospel debate and the discussion of what is entailed in a functioning priesthood of all believers.

There are dangers in writing history. One can *revise* history in order to make it fit a desired pattern; or one could *romanticize* history in order to glorify a particular tradition. I have tried to be objective with the facts, and have made only a few interpretive observations.

It must be stressed at the outset that I love and respect those mentioned in the course of this essay. In reporting and commenting past events, I only wish to contribute to a *Christ-centered* discussion of issues, and to encourage others to maintain an *open stance* toward one another. If disappointment over the beliefs and actions of others is expressed, it is done in a context of full acceptance of these brethren.

1. THE LAW/GOSPEL DEBATE

"God's Covenants"

It was in 1967, while at Bob Jones University, that I came to believe that the Lord's Gospel was God-centered, not man-centered. I transferred to Covenant College in 1968. My reading during the period of 1968-1973 was "Puritan/Reformed" in emphasis.

My pointed reflection on the law/gospel issue began around 1972. Greg Hufstetler and I were alternating on the chapters of the 1742 *Philadelphia Confession of Faith* in the Sunday School of Sovereign Grace Baptist Church in Prospectville, PA. The chapter "Of God's Covenant" fell on my shoulders.

After an in-depth study of that chapter, I presented

two lessons: "Covenants and the O.T." and "Covenants in the N.T." I fully expected to be thrown out of the church, for I not only rejected the Dispensationalist interpretation which stressed *discontinuity* in God's program, but I also felt compelled to reject the one *'Covenant of Grace'* (continuity) position of Covenant Theology. I concluded that neither system did justice to the biblical data, and that both systems had to skip over or twist much Scripture in order to sustain their positions. Happily, the listeners (including about ten students from Westminster Seminary) were open to what I taught, and thought that the questions I'd raised were worth further investigation.

After these two Sunday School lessons, my thought was not stimulated again on this subject until the publication of E.W. Johnson's article on "Imputation" (*BRR*, 3:2, Summer, 1974, 21-45).

Is There A "Covenant of Grace"?

I wrote a response, "Reflections on E.W. Johnson's 'Imputation' Article" in *BRR*, 4:1, 1975, pp. 57-62. The preparing of this study brought me to again face some issues in "Federal Theology." In a passing remark, I agreed with E.W. Johnson's reservations about the "Covenant of Redemption."

> Specifically, however, it should be acknowledged that his point is especially well taken regarding the alleged "covenant of redemption"…As theologians have presented this "covenant of grace," they have simply posited its existence, and have not shown its presence in the Bible. There is an eternal purpose of God in Christ Jesus, and there are historical covenants revealed in Scripture. But a "covenant of grace" which stands above history does not appear to be a Scriptural concept ("Reflections," p. 57).

Thoughts on this subject were not aroused again until several years later when I finally read a book that had been on my shelf for years, *The Reformers and Their Stepchildren.*

While living in Philadelphia, I traveled to Wilmington, DE, in 1969 to visit Puritan-Reformed Book Service—then operating out of Walt Hibbard's garage! Walt pressed me to purchase Leonard Verduin's *The Reformers and Their Stepchildren* (Eerdmans, 1964). I reluctantly bought it, and it sat on a shelf until June, 1977, when—at the urging of several brothers earlier in the year—I read it carefully.

This book was singularly helpful to me. It cleared a lot of fog out of my head, and the pieces of theology and church history that I'd been wrestling with since 1969 began to fall together. Verduin conclusively showed two things: (1) the visible church since Constantine was informed more by the old than the new covenant; (2) the issue between the Catholics/ Protestants and the Anabaptists was a radically different conception of "what the church of Christ is and what its relation is to that which lies around it" (Reformers, p. 16; cf. pp. 23, 38, 50, 54).

The reading of *Reformers* confirmed to me that something needed to be said about the issues of law/grace and a "believing church."

"The First Shot Fired in Twenty Years"

I prepared a manuscript and sent it to seven respected brothers before it was published. Only a few responded. The article—which John Reisinger called "the first shot fired in twenty years"—asked the penetrating question, "Is There A 'Covenant of Grace'?" It appeared in the Autumn, 1977, *BRR.* This article was to initiate heated discussion, and even bitter controversy.

Some positive responses were generated. The only negative written reply came from a Westminster Seminary student, and this was printed in the Spring, 1978, *BRR*, along with my follow-up article, "Crucial Thoughts On 'Law' in the New Covenant."

"Neo-dispensationalism" and "Neo-antinomianism"?

In 1978 and 1979 the opposition to the articles in *BRR* accelerated (accompanied also by a number of positive encouragements!). Walt Chantry, a leader among the "Reformed Baptists" in the northeast, wrote a brief letter and accused me (without providing any documentation) of propagating "neo-dispensationalism" and "neo-antinomianism" (July, 1978).

I spent hours at the Vanderbilt Library in Nashville researching "antinomianism," and documented in my lengthy reply to Walt why I repudiated it. I re-sent Walt my articles that disturbed him, and asked him to underline any sentences that bothered him, and told him that I would be glad to consider any points he wished to make (August, 1978). No reply was ever received.

Discovering the Anabaptists

You don't hear much about the Anabaptists in the standard church histories—and when mentioned, they are often portrayed as "heretics." It is ironic that men who have been quick to label Anabaptist excesses as "fanatical" are so slow to apply the same label to the Catholics and Protestants who murdered people for their non-compliance with established religion.

The Autumn, 1978, *BRR* was devoted to acquainting people with a heritage that was far ahead of its times in certain areas. Subsequent history showed that "The Stepchildren (Anabaptists) were heading in the right direction and their opponents in the wrong" (G.R. Beasley-Murray, "Postscript," *Reformers* [Paternoster], p. 277). In the two areas of focus here (law and ministry), the Anabaptists broke with the past and asserted: (1) that there was a *new* covenant with Christ as its focus and norm; and (2) that there was a new community in Christ which could assemble and function in simplicity. The Anabaptists had faults; but we err not to profit from the insights which cost them their lives.

"This Is My Beloved Son, Hear Him"

I pursued research on law/gospel at Vanderbilt for months. I read thousands of pages on "Christian Ethics." Something was missing. The bulk of the treatments simply saw ethics as an exposition of the Ten Commandments. I asked the Lord to guide me to a book that would have some insight into this matter. Not long after, I found A.J. Bandstra's *The Law and the Elements of the World: An Exegetical Study in Aspects of Paul's Teaching* (Kok, 1964). This was a breakthrough for me. Then, while at Westminster in December of 1978, I came upon F.F. Bruce's *Paul: Apostle of the Heart Set Free*. This book further confirmed that the direction I was heading in was not unique.

In 1978 I had received a negative letter from Don Garlington, who was then teaching at Trinity Ministerial Academy in New Jersey. I met with Don for a few hours at the Mariott Hotel in Saddlebrook, New Jersey, in December of 1978. First, we discussed his letter and he agreed to modify the ending for publication. Then I read to him some quotations from Samuel Bolton's *The True Bounds of Christian*

Freedom, and asked him if he felt that these Puritan remarks reflected sensitivity to N.T. teaching. He agreed that Bolton's statements were not entirely accurate. I felt that he was between a rock and a hard place, knowing that the Puritan view had some problems, yet teaching in a school where Puritanism had to be upheld.

In January, 1979, I prepared a lengthy manuscript and sent it out to about twenty-five people with a request for feedback. Many encouraging remarks were received in response to "My Beloved Son."

In the Winter, 1978, *BRR,* eight positive responses and the negative letter from Don Garlington were printed as lead-ins to my article, "This Is My Beloved Son, Hear Him: A Study of the Development of Law in the History of Redemption." This was my most exhaustive attempt to set forth a Christ-centered approach to ethics.

"I was almost a Presbyterian"
In October, 1978, I spoke with Thom Smith at the Banner of Truth Conference in Atlanta. In April, 1979, Thom called me and apologized for giving me the "cold shoulder." Further, he told me that he had re-read the articles in *BRR,* and felt that I was possibly opening the way for a consistent "Baptist theology." His theology changed significantly as the months rolled on, as did the thinking of his close friend, Ron McKinney.

I didn't realize it at the time, but when I had written Thom a letter in early 1979 he was undergoing much theological turmoil, and was almost to the point of becoming a Presbyterian. Reflecting on the one-two punch effect of a very providential plane trip with John Reisinger and my letter, Thom said in October, 1979:

I got home and Jon Zens had written me a letter and just took me apart…*very* kind, *very* gentle. I'll tell you, Jon has been a Christian through all the muck and dung that has been slung on him in the past six months to a year. He's really shown a Christian spirit in it all. His letter savored of the breath of Christ (Men's Meeting, Reformed Baptist Church of Dallas, 10/19/79).

"He almost made me a Baptist!"

In January, 1979, I traveled from Nashville to a preacher's fellowship in Dalton, Ga., where John Reisinger and Ferrell Griswold were to speak on law-related subjects. I went with fear and trembling, wondering if I would be shunned. John's exposition of Galatians 3 and 4 was excellent. He opened his talk by asking how many present read *BRR*—a few hands went up. He then mentioned the significance he felt was attached to my article on the "Covenant of Grace," and commented that my editorial, "What Can We Learn From Reformation History?" "almost made me a Baptist!"

"Paul did not follow the reasoning of BRR"

At the Summer, 1979, Reformed Baptist Family Conference Walt Chantry delivered some messages on the "Kingdom of God." In them he attacked the positions of the Reconstructionist movement and *BRR*. Walt suggested that our position carried with it a denial that there is only one people of God and one way of salvation, a denial that the O.T. is relevant for now, and a denial that the heathen are sinners (because they are not "under law"). While he quoted from the Reconstructionists, he never once cited anything from *BRR* to document his strong (and wrong) accusations.

In my reply to these tapes (August, 1979), I tried to show Walt that he had totally misconstrued what I believed. Since Al Martin introduced these tapes by announcing that the substance of Walt's messages would be put into book form, I pleaded with Walt in my reply to not go into print with these misrepresentations of my position.

Walt replied, but still made no attempt to document his allegations (September, 1979). His displeasure was obvious:

> It is clear that some major shifts have been made. And your new categories have sown confusion in our churches—not about what we shall call Biblical teachings. Your writings have provoked a new revolt against the very Biblical idea of righteousness and altered the Biblical understanding of the gospel...What has been put into print has been damaging to the cause of Christ...With complete distaste for controversy, but with greater aversion to your dangerous and confusing novelties, Walter J. Chantry, Pastor.

"Cranks who foment against Sinai"

In 1980 Walt's book appeared, *God's Righteous Kingdom*. While in the tapes he named names, the book doesn't—the reader is left to figure out who the two "enemies" are. In the course of this book, he continues to brandish outlandish claims: "others argue that no moral law applicable to Christians may be found in the O.T."; "Sinaiphobia which would eliminate any Mosaic code as invalid for N.T. times"; "others wish only to be rid of anything Moses touched"; "cranks who foment against Sinai."

In response, I said in part:

> I am also disconcerted and hurt when someone with undocumented pontification utterly misrepresents my convictions (especially after I pleaded with you not to

misrepresent me before you went into print)…I am at a loss to know what else to say, for my previous letters to you have expressed parallel concerns, yet you have gone on with your unloving, unscholarly course (December 1, 1980).

In his reply, he did finally give some quotations from my writings, but they certainly did not begin to substantiate the colored language used in the book.. "For substantiation of what I have to say, I could almost quote the entirety of the articles that you have printed in *BRR"* (December 10, 1980).

The Birth of the Council on Baptist Theology

At the fall Banner of Truth Conference in 1979, Ron McKinney spoke with Iain Murray, Ernie Reisinger and others about the possibility of having a conference where some aspects of Reformed theology could be discussed and evaluated by people of differing viewpoints. The answer was "No"—unless Banner of Truth had control of who would speak and what topics would be addressed. Ron found this unacceptable. After talking with others, the idea was born for a conference where traditions could be discussed and evaluated, and Ron began to make plans for the Summer "1980 Council on Baptist Theology" to be held in Plano, TX.

Ron McKinney called me in January of 1980 and asked if I would speak at the Council in May. My subject would be "An Examination of the Presuppositions of Covenant and Dispensational Theology."

The conference was well-attended, there was a good spirit among the attendees, the topics dealt with were refreshing and edifying, and discussion was encouraged. It was gratifying to me to see the Lord Jesus lifted up in the New Covenant, and to see so many brethren rejoicing in (and wrestling with) the issues we had sought to unfold in *BRR*.

"'As I Have Loved You': The Starting Point of Christian Obedience" *(BRR*, 9:2, 1980) was brought to this conference and was well-received.

A Man on a Pilgrimage: RDB

I started receiving *Present Truth* (later *Verdict)* at Westminster Seminary (1972). I didn't read it much, however, until 1975. The emphasis on justification was helpful to me at this time.

In August, 1979—through a series of fluke circumstances—I heard about some unadvertised meetings at a Ramada Inn in Nashville. For three days the editor of *Verdict,* Robert D. Brinsmead, was addressing about 150 Adventist-oriented people. I came Friday night and spoke with RDB and Jack Zwemer in their motel room for about two hours. We also talked for another two hours on Sunday night.

I was impressed by Brinsmead's teachable, open spirit. He obviously did not feel threatened by my pointed and probing questions. One area that I asked him about was the idea that the law had to do a "work" before the gospel could come to folks. His magazine had been permeated with this concept. I suggested that if all things are to be approached through Christ, why do we put the law ahead of Him in evangelism? Where in Acts were the Ten Commandments preached before the gospel? He said he thought I had some good points and that he would reflect upon them. On Sunday night I gave him Richard Gaffin's *The Centrality of the Resurrection,* Meredith Kline's *The Structure of Biblical Authority,* and all of the back issues of *BRR*.

In January, 1980, Brinsmead called from California, just

before he was to leave for Australia. He said that he had read the back issues, that he thought we were on to something important, and that he would study these matters closely in Australia.

In 1981 some brilliant essays appeared in *Verdict*. "Sabbatarianism Re-examined," "Jesus and the Law," and "The Heart of N.T. Ethics" presented a Christ-centered approach to ethics. It was certainly heartening to see this shift by the largest English-speaking theological journal in the world at that time (sadly, since mid-1984 RDB went markedly downhill).

"Wild Bulls Propagating Classic Antinomianism"

In February of 1980, Al Martin presented an emotionally charged message on "Law and Gospel" to a pastors' fellowship in Canada. In it he echoed the charges Waif Chantry—"neo-antinomianism," "*de facto* dispensationalism," "nothing is regulative for the Christian but the N.T. documents," "Moses no longer has any valid function in the church of Jesus Christ."

In my March 25, 1980, reply to Pastor Martin, I had to ask him just how he would document his sweeping charges, and why he had to resort to such highly charged emotionalism (e.g., saying that we encouraged people to "stop their ears to Moses," and "they go on like wild bulls propagating their views of classic antinomianism"). I further said:

> As Pastor D.M. Canright said, "men who are conscious of being in the right can afford to state the position of their opponents fairly."…You do your position no help by saying that *BRR* has put a "concrete barrier" between the two Testaments, and that "nothing is carried over." No, Pastor Martin, such biased sentiments cannot be documented in *BRR*. If your position is right, then please manifest a

Christian, brotherly approach in stating the position of your opponents fairly (3/25/80).

No reply was ever received from Pastor Martin.

One of the pastors who attended this presentation in Toronto, James Shantz, wrote a letter to Al Martin in which he said, "I continue to be greatly dismayed by your lecture on Law and Grace, as I have continued to study it on tape. Your declaration that *BRR*...is teaching antinomianism reveals that you yourself have not carefully studied all the materials." Further, Shantz wrote a lengthy paper, "The Puritan Giant and the Antinomian 'Ghost,'" in which he raised a number of questions about traditional Reformed theology.

The Sabbath and Other Matters

During the period of 1979-1980, *BRR* devoted much space to the foundations of N.T. ethics. Both the Spring and Winter 1979 issues dealt with the relationship of law and gospel. Bob Morey asked, "Is Sunday the 'Christian Sabbath'?," and Albertus Pieters (a paedobaptist leader in the Reformed Church of America in the 1940's) showed much insight about the place of the Ten Commandments in the history of redemption in "The Seed of Abraham and the Old Covenant" (Spring, 1979). I dealt with "Principles of New Covenant Giving" (Summer, 1979), W.B. Selbie investigated "The Influence of the O.T. On Puritanism" (Autumn, 1979), and Don Price interacted with the attempts to connect an *imperative* to Sunday worship (Winter, 1980).

A sort of (unintended) culmination occurred in the Spring, 1981, *BRR*. There were lengthy review articles of Walt Chantry's *God's Righteous Kingdom* and Robert Brinsmead's *Judged by the Gospel: A Review of Adventism*. The dynamic

N.T. approach to law and gospel was stated forcefully by RDB:

> [Paul's] appeals on how to live are made on the basis of what God has done for us in Christ. It is in view of God's gospel mercies that we are to present our lives as a living sacrifice to God (Rom. 12:1-3)…Paul virtually never appeals to the law—'Thou shalt not.' When he demands certain behavior of the church, he appeals instead to the holy history of Christ…and from that standpoint then makes his ethical appeal. (p. 6)

Regarding "the gospel and the church," I stated: George Wolfgang Forell makes astute observations about the tragic shift from mutual ministry to unilateral dominion in the early church:

> Ethical guidance for people recently converted to Christianity and likely to bring a pervasive pagan attitude to this new life was offered at first by a polyform ministry of grace, reflected in the N.T. But as time went by moral authority was increasingly focused in an ordered ministry of bishops and deacons *(History of Christian Ethics,* I, 39).

I personally have come to the conviction that the greatest practical need facing the church today is the recovery of the *"polyform ministry of grace"* (p. 8).

As *BRR* from 1981 onwards began to assert the obvious disparity between the "polyform" ministry found in the N.T. and the "ordered system" of various post-apostolic traditions, then even those who agreed with our New Covenant orientation began to be displeased and concerned. This leads us to the historical overview of the second topic, "ministry in the church."

2. WHAT IS INVOLVED IN A FUNCTIONING PRIESTHOOD?

In the course of the shared teaching ministry we had at Sovereign Grace Baptist Church (Prospectville, Pa., 1972-1973), I brought several studies on Hebrews 3 and 10. I began to see that *mutual exhortation* was embedded in what was called "the perseverance of the saints" (Heb. 3:6,14). Yet, in all of my reading of the standard Calvinistic treatises on the believer's security, I *never* saw the Hebrews' passages connected with "final perseverance." Perseverance was approached in an *individualistic* manner—those given by God to Christ will be finally saved, and none will be lost. This is very true, but I never saw the *corporate* (body) dimension developed as a key means in our "working out" of salvation. Several years later I would come to see *why* this was the case: since the edification of the church was placed on the shoulders of one man—"the minister"—the "ministry" of the saints one with another was not practiced.

A Penetrating Question

After moving to Nashville in 1975, I came into contact with a "house church" in 1976. One of its members, Ken Leary, and I decided to meet regularly and work our way through Louis Berkhof's *The History of Christian Doctrines*. One day something in our study provoked Ken to ask me, "Where does the N.T. teach that 'preaching' must be central in a service—like it is in your church?" I was upset by his "impertinent" question, and gave him the pat-answer I had been taught—"1 Cor. 1:21 teaches that it is through the foolishness of preaching that people are saved." Ken was not satisfied with my remarks, suggested that 'preaching' seemed to take place 'outside' the church in evangelism, and the subject was dropped. However, his question kept echoing in my mind.

I was struck with the message of 1 Timothy 3:15, and the next step in my ecclesiological pilgrimage took place when I wrote "The Local Church: The Pillar and Ground of the Truth" (*BRR*, Summer, 1977). This booklet was apparently a blessing and a challenge to many. John Alexander, then president of InterVarsity Christian Fellowship, requested 100 copies to distribute among those in that organization.

The subject of ecclesiology—the doctrine of the church—became a matter of intense research. The Summer, 1978, *BRR* was devoted to "Church Government" and "Eldership in the N.T." A number expressed appreciation for Mike Parker's article on "The Basic Meaning of 'Elder' in the N.T." One pattern that emerged from the N.T. was the *plural* nature of oversight in the local church. The traditional one pastor practice appeared to be untenable.

"One Man or One Another?"

My stance on the local church was further challenged in 1979. I remember the day Al Lewis—who had moved from Wyoming to be part of our church in Nashville—sat down with me and lovingly shared some ideas from 1 Corinthinans 14 about how an assembly should function together. Again, I was driven to re-think some issues.

By December, 1979, I had completed a rough draft of an article, "Building Up the Body: One Man or One Another?" I initially sent out 65 copies of it with a cover letter requesting feedback, and by March, 1980, about 125 copies had been circulated. The feedback rolled in—positive, negative and mixed. Some felt that it should not be published until down the road—one pastor suggested three or four years! It was obviously a sensitive issue, in some crucial ways more touchy than the law/gospel debate. Hence the concern for feedback before it was published.

The sensitive nature of this article was highlighted by a phone call I received from Ron McKinney in April, 1980. He asked me if I was going to publish "One Man or One Another" immediately. I replied that I fully intended to publish it, but in the future, after the feedback was in and I had time to reflect on and digest it. He was glad, and related that if it's publication was imminent a number of men felt that I should not be allowed to speak at the upcoming "1980 Council on Baptist Theology."

As it turned out, "Building Up the Body" was published in the Summer, 1981, *BRR*—a year and a half after the rough draft was circulated. Before publishing it, I carefully weighed the criticisms in light of Scripture, and incorporated a number of helpful comments and changes in the final draft.

As a follow-up to "Building Up the Body," the Autumn, 1981, issue developed some "Aspects of Female Priesthood (1 Cor. 11-14)" in response to questions raised by the first article.

Movement Toward An "Association"
After the 1981 Council on Baptist Theology some felt that forming a Baptist association was in order. In 1981 I received an invitation to attend a steering committee meeting in Richardson, Texas, at the end of November. Several papers would be presented, and there was to be open discussion about the advisability and feasibility of forming an association.

One attitude that surfaced at this meeting several times concerned me deeply. In his opening remarks, Ron McKinney stated his conviction that "we will be a flash in the pan of church history unless we get together." John Armstrong stated in his paper that if we do not have revival and missions outreach (in the context, through an association), "I fear that we shall at best be relegated, and rightly so, to a brief footnote at best, in the Baptist history being written in our day." I got the feeling that an underlying motive for creating an association was "to be something."

"Problems in Our Churches"

After John Armstrong's presentation on the evening of December 1, Thom Smith asked if I would have a meeting with several men. John's paper had already expressed discontent with *BRR*—"our persistence in writing about 'new ideas' and 'challenging the brethren' to correct this mistaken practice or that…will we keep 'going our own way' writing our articles and papers on issues that divide our churches and create new 'fires for pastors to spend time extinguishing'?"

In this meeting with eight men, Thom opened by expressing appreciation for the help *BRR* had been in the law/gospel discussion, but felt that the "body-life" teaching found in the magazine was not in line with Baptist tradition, and was causing division in some churches. Seven of the eight men then proceeded to express their reservations, and gave alleged examples of where *BRR* articles had caused problems in churches. No attempt was made in this meeting to show that what was said in *BRR* was *against Christ;* it was just assumed to be in error, and not in line with Baptist doctrine. The fact that something "causes trouble" is not sufficient grounds for it to be *wrong.*

In the days following the meeting I investigated the three incidents cited, and was satisfied that the "trouble" was not our fault. The people involved were certainly appalled that blame would be imputed to me or the magazine.

"Searching Together"

In the Spring, 1982, *BRR* I asked if it was appropriate for "Baptists" to be "Reformed." But brother Glynn Taylor wrote and asked if it was right for Christians to call themselves "Baptists"—or anything else that only highlighted factions in the body of Christ.

In 1981 and 1982 I was privileged to speak at several West Coast *Verdict* seminars. Here, I met a number of former Seventh-Day Adventists. During these times it became evident that the title of our magazine was a hindrance to people getting into its contents. It was the kind of situation where you end up spending your time explaining what you are *not*.

This consideration, coupled with the facts that our readership was broadening, and that the ministry was not intended only for "Baptists," led to a name change: *Searching Together*. This name—based on Eph. 4:15 and Acts 17:11—expresses our innermost desire to pursue Christ in fellowship with others.

THE NEED: TO FOCUS ON CHRIST TOGETHER

Our Spring, 1983, issue said some things about what churches need most. I believe that the "controversy" over law/gospel and ministry in the church over the past seven years illustrates (negatively) what we need most. All the fuss, gossip and bad attitudes among the brethren can be attributed to a lack of *maturity* and to a great deal of *insecurity*. These two serious problems can be spiritually dealt with by the following five points.

1. *Christ must be the beginning, middle, and end of everything.* As Vernard Eller said in 1964, Christ "is the supreme revelation and the very presence of God himself." It's not about being right, being Baptist (or any thing else), having the right church government, having the right order of service, or having the best theology. *If it isn't about the living Christ we might as well eat, drink, be merry and die tomorrow.*

2. We need an *unqualified acceptance* of one another in the gospel (Rom. 15:7). We need to realize that our very titles ("can we admit a church into our association that does not have 'Baptist' in its name?") in reality keep us from accepting others. We end up in practice accepting others "if..." Commitment to any "tradition" ends up clouding the gospel for we are then forced to defend the indefensible.

    Traditional Adventism appeals to its unique doctrines as the only justification for its existence. In this it is not unlike Lutheranism, Calvinism, Campbellism [Church of Christ] or other branches of the church. Each group tends to cling to its special contribution as if that justified its existence. And generally the special contribution overwhelms the New Testament message. The only thing which justifies our right to exist either individually or corporately is the gospel. The reason why Adventism cannot face the truth of history but has created so many pious legends [as other groups have] is that it depends upon that history for its corporate justification. Yet right here it unwittingly expresses its denial of justification by Christ alone. Only one history justifies our right to exist either individually or corporately—the holy history of Jesus of Nazareth. To embrace the gospel means that we confess that all history but Christ's stands under the judgment. It is His history plus nothing which justifies our existence." (Robert D. Brinsmead, *Judged by the Gospel*, pp. 325, 359).

3. We need *non-threatening atmospheres* in our churches. Only with unqualified acceptance can we then express Christ freely to one another (Rom. 15:14). Too many people in churches are intimidated, confused and scared. A letter recently received illustrates the tragedy of this problem:

> As the Lord appointed us to grow through suffering and through knowledge of His Son, we all come to face problems. I want to mention a problem I have now. I hope you will understand, and maybe give me some biblical light to see the problem in a realistic way and learn from it. The problem is this. I have been going to a Baptist church for six years. As I have grown in knowledge, I have come to believe that the teaching emphasis in this church is unbiblical. They teach tithing, Sabbath-keeping, and the love of God is presented as 'grace under law.' Feeling unfed by the elders, I don't know if I should stop being among them. Should I stay and give my viewpoints according to Scripture? Sometimes in Sunday school I ask questions and they go unanswered; sometimes I explain a subject and silence is my answer. So what do I do, leave or stay?

4. We need *open agendas*. The reason letters like this can be written is because the agenda is predefined and

prepackaged in most churches. If someone raises a question that is outside of the accepted parameters, they are "dealt with."

If truth is a *growing* thing in our experience then, as Vernard Eller notes, "no group ever has the 'last word,' and must always be eager and open for new leading rather than complacent in knowledge already attained."

In 1978 many brethren thought I was a "troubler in Israel" when I started teaching a Christ-centered ethic. But they hung in there with me, and as time went on many began to see some light.

However, I believe some of these same brethren have since 1981 closed their mind to further light regarding what is involved in a functioning priesthood. I am now viewed as one disturbing the status quo. Would they be willing to work though a book like Howard Snyder's *The Problem of Wineskins,* or is the agenda closed?

When one pastor told me that my teachings were not in line with "Baptist tradition," you can see that for him the agenda was already fixed. This is the problem: commitment to *one* tradition (1) makes certain topics "taboo"; (2) allows study of "approved" topics only; (3) effectively seals a group off from learning valuable truth from the "other guys"—who are usually viewed as the "bad guys" (non-acceptance).

5. We need the *ability to work through things with other believers*. It is my observation that this is the biggest lack in churches (and is a consequence of serious lacks in the first four areas mentioned above). *Most churches have no spiritual mechanisms* by which to handle (1) new aspects

of truth that naturally come up in church life, (2) inter-personal conflicts, (3) "loose ends" in relationships and teachings, which have a tendency to backlog in churches.

The *problem* cannot be located strictly in right or wrong views of law/gospel or the priesthood of believers—important as these matters are. Paul locates our greatest needs in Eph. 4:1-3 "walk in a manner worthy of the calling with which you have been called, with all humility and gentleness, with patience, showing forbearance to one another in love, being diligent to preserve the unity of the Spirit in the bond of peace." Vernard Eller puts his finger on some key issues:

The preservation of fellowship is the precondition for the reception and preservation of religious truth…Much more important than *having* the truth is being in a position to *receive* the truth.

Unless we see some radical improvement regarding these five areas, we have no reason to expect the situation in churches to get better. We must learn to work through the difficult times together in a setting of acceptance. Otherwise, there can be no doubt but that we will go on biting and devouring one another.

May the Lord Jesus help us in the future to see significant growth in these four areas. ∎

Books for further reading:

1. D.L. Baker, *Two Testaments: One Bible* (IVP, 1977).

2. A.J. Bandstra, *The Law & the Elements of the World: An Exegetical Study in Aspects of Paul's Theology* (Kok, 1964), 210pp.

3. Robert Banks, *Paul's Idea of Community: The Early House Churches in Their Historical Setting* (Eerdmans, 1980).

4. Robert Brinsmead, "Jesus & the Law," *Verdict,* 4:6, Oct., 1981;

5. "Sabbatarianism Re-examined," June, 1981; "The Heart of N.T. Ethics," Jan., 1982.

6. F.F. Bruce, *Paul: Apostle of the Heart Set Free* (Eerdmans, 1977).

7. Steve Carpenter, "Paul, the Law, and Redemptive History," 1981 Council on Baptist Theology, 38pp.

8. Richard Gaffin, *The Centrality of the Resurrection* (Baker, 1978).

9. Meredith Kline, *The Structure of Biblical Authority* (Eerdmans, 1975).

10. Richard Longenecker, *Paul, Apostle of Liberty* (Baker, 1980); *The Ministry and Message of Paul* (Zondervan, 1981).

11. Mark McCulley, "Baptist Reformation Review," *Studies in History & Ethics,* 108pp.

12. Larry Richards (C. Hoeldtke), *A Theology of Church Leadership* (Zondervan, 1980); Richards (G. Martin), *A Theology of Personal Ministry* (Zondervan, 1981). A one-two punch that is hard to beat!

13. James Shantz, "The Puritan Giant & the Antinomian 'Ghost'," 15pp.

14. Howard Snyder, *The Community of the King* & *The Problem of Wineskins* (IVP)

15. Leonard Verduin, *The Reformers & Their Stepchildren* (Eerdmans, 1964).

16. John H. Yoder, "Binding & Loosing," *Concern #14* (Feb., 1967).

17. Jon Zens, *Is There A 'Covenant of Grace?'* [1977]/*Crucial Thoughts On 'Law' in the New Covenant* [1978], 22pp.

EXCERPTS FROM *STUDIES IN THEOLOGY AND ETHICS*

JON ZENS, 1981

1977 was a pivotal year for me. After visiting a radical assembly in February I was challenged to read The Reformers & Their Stepchildren *(Leonard Verduin) and then* The Problem of Wineskins *(Howard Snyder). I began to see that the dominant systems of Covenant Theology and Dispensationalism were fraught with serious problems. As various circumstances converged, a Council on Baptist Theology was held in mid-1980 in Plano, Texas. I was asked to present a plenary paper, and it was titled, "An Examination of the Presuppositions of Covenant and Dispensational Theology." It created quite a stir! It was put into a book titled* Studies in Theology & Ethics, *which was published in 1981. What follows are selections from that book.*

INTRODUCTION

"With Christ's advent the law, also as far as its content is concerned, has been brought under a new norm of judgment and…failure to appreciate this new situation is a denial of Christ (Gal. 5:2)…The application of the commandment to love consequently has in Paul the clear effect of stirring up the strong awareness in the church of mutual responsibility…The particularizing of this love constitutes a large part of the content of the Pauline paraenesis [ethic]." (Herman Ridderbos. *Paul: An Outline of His Theology*, pp. 294, 297.)

"We must say that the Bible has no independent interest in ethics. If God wanted to provide a manual on ethical conduct, He could have easily done so. But the Bible is not an ethical manual any more than it is a systematic theology. The Bible is written as history. It is a story of God's redemptive acts. Biblical ethics are not artificially attached to this story. They are embedded in the story itself…When biblical ethics are removed from the context of redemptive history, they cease to be biblical ethics. In this respect Judeo-Christian ethics are absolutely unique. They cannot be duplicated by anyone not incorporated into the holy history of Israel—a history which has climaxed in Jesus Christ. As far as the Bible is concerned, ethics have no independent value and no meaning outside the saving deeds of God.…

[Paul's] appeals on how to live are made on the basis of what God has done for us in Christ. It is in view of God's gospel mercies that we are to present our lives as a living sacrifice to God. (Rom. 12:1-3)…Paul virtually never appeals to the law—'Thou shalt not.' When he demands certain behavior of the church, he appeals instead to the holy history of Christ, into which the church is incorporated, and from that standpoint then makes his ethical

SEARCHING TOGETHER | FALL-WINTER 2018

appeal...." (Robert D. Brinsmead. *Judged by the Gospel*, pp. 209, 213.)

"It is too easy for us to romanticize some portions of post-apostolic history. We glory in being 'Baptists,' 'Adventists,' 'Presbyterians,' or any other group. The history of *our* heritage then becomes something we must 'defend'—even if it is wrong. But we must rise above this sectarian mentality. And there is *one* consideration that will surely accomplish this: 'consider the Apostle and High Priest of our confession, Christ Jesus' (Heb. 3:1). The only history above reproach is the *history of Christ.*

Traditional Adventism appeals to its unique doctrines as the only justification for its existence. In this it is not unlike Lutheranism, Calvinism, Campbellism or other branches of the church. Each group tends to cling to its special contribution as if that justified its existence. And generally the special contribution overwhelms the New Testament message. The only thing which justifies our right to exist either individually or corporately is the gospel...Only one history justifies our right to exist...the holy history of Jesus of Nazareth. To embrace the gospel means that we confess that all history but Christ's stands under the judgment of God. It is His history plus nothing which justifies our existence...the gospel demands that we find the justification for our existence in the history of Jesus Christ alone. (*Judged by the Gospel.* pp. 325, 359).

CONCERNS RELATED TO DISPENSATIONALISM

Acts 28:17, 20, 23—"For the hope of Israel I am bound with this chain..."

What is this "hope" for which Paul was bound? "The only hope answering to the description, as an ancient, national, and still intense one, is the hope of the Messiah" (J.A. Alexander, A *Commentary on the Acts of the Apostles*, ll, p. 412: cf. Acts 26:6-7). Thus it was Paul's "Messianic doctrine that had caused the breach between him and his countrymen" (*Ibid.* p. 486). This "hope" also embraced the future resurrection of the just and unjust.

There is nothing to suggest in Paul's testimonies that the "hope" of Israel is *future*, except with respect to the resurrection (24:15) which has just been fulfilled by Christ in the recent *past*. The hope of future resurrection is based on the accomplished resurrection of Christ. Paul's point is that the "hope" of Israel has come. On this foundation he proclaimed from the O.T. Scriptures "that Christ should suffer and that he should be the first to rise from the dead, and should show light to the Gentiles" (26:22—23). Since their "hope" had come, it was Paul's intense desire to see Israel "saved" (Rom. 10:1) and "converted" by the gospel (Acts 28:27).

Romans 8:19-24—"For the earnest expectation of the creation waits for the manifestation of the sons of God…the adoption, the redemption of our body…"

Ryrie states that "the goal of history is the earthly millennium… this millennial culmination is the climax of history and the great goal of God's program for the ages" (*Dispensationalism Today*. pp. 18, 104).

But these texts assert that the goal for which the creation awaits is not a millennium, but the "adoption, the redemption of our body." Thus, the entire creation is groaning for the consummation of the *church*, that is, the glorification of the saints. Notice that deliverance from corruption (the curse) is coterminous with the glorious liberty of the saints. How then can the goal of the creation be an "earthly millennium" which is, according to dispensationalists, essentially Jewish?

CONCERNS RELATED TO COVENANT THEOLOGY

Many theologians teach that Christ was subordinate to the Father before history, and that is why He was subordinate to Him in history. Where does the Scripture reveal this rationale for why the Word was made flesh? It would be my judgment that their elaborations of the "covenant of redemption" caused them to bring the proper subordination of the Son in the historical economy of salvation into the pre-temporal Trinitarian relationship.

The verse that has been used in a confusing manner in this regard is Psalm 2:7—"I will declare the decree: the Lord has said to me, you are my Son; this day have I begotten you." This verse has been used with reference to an *eternal* relationship of Father and Son (cf. Heppe, p. 120). However, it is clear that the verse itself refers to a decree to be realized in history, not to an *eternal relationship*. Further, the N.T. quotes this verse several times (Acts 13:33; Heb. 1:4-5). In these places, Ps. 2:7 is clearly referenced to the *historical manifestation* (and, more pointedly, to the resurrection) of Christ, not to the *eternal relationship* of Father and Son. R.C.H. Lenski noted on Acts 13:33:

> The passage occurring in the Psalm does not speak of the *generatio aeterna*, not of the inner Trinitarian relation of the two Persons, not of eternity but of time (*Interpretation of Acts*, p. 538).

The verses used to substantiate an *eternal subordination* of the Son in fact refer to the relationship of the Trinity in the *outworking of redemption in history* (cf. Heppe, pp. 118-121).

Verses that relate to God's action in history are wrongly applied to the pre-temporal relationship of the Trinity. It is of critical importance to distinguish between the *pre-temporal* relationship and the *economic* (historical) relationship of the Trinity. Psalm 2:7 falls in the latter category; a verse like John 15:5b falls in the former category.

The Covenant of Grace and Church/State Union

Historically, covenant theology has been connected with the ideal of a "Christian state," or "holy commonwealth" (cf. Leonard Verduin. *The Reformers and Their Stepchildren*, and *Anatomy of A Hybrid;* Jon Zens, "'More of Cromwell, Less of Gurnall'?" *Baptist Reformation Review*, 8:1, 1979, pp. 20-32; W.B. Selbie. "The Influence of the Old Testament On Puritanism," *BRR*, 8:3, 1979).

Some contemporary men, such as Drs. R.J. Rushdoony and Greg Bahnsen, are calling for covenant theologians to evidence consistency by returning to the strong "holy commonwealth" ideals of the 1646 Westminster Assembly (cf. Bahnsen, "God's Law and Gospel Prosperity: A Reply to the Editor of the Presbyterian Journal," pp. 10, 12, 29).

The Reformers and the Puritans, unfortunately, believed it was justifiable to employ the sword in the maintenance of "true religion." The O.T had to be their textbook in this regard (De Jong, p. 80: "much of the political theory of the Puritans was derived directly from the Old Testament"). H. Bullinger, Zwingli's assistant, was typical of their attitude when he said "the Christian emperors a 1000 years ago were right to appoint capital punishment for those who should spread new dogma and teach different things with insult to God [about the Trinity]" (quoted by Heppe, p. 105).

While later covenant theology came to believe that church and state should be separate in principle, "in practice this did not happen" (De Jong, p. 79). De Jong sees the rejection of the "theocratic ideal which had inspired first [New England] fathers" as a significant contributing factor to the decline of Calvinism (p. 9).

John Warick Montgomery seems to pinpoint the connection of the *one* covenant concept and church/state union:

The most influential factor in creating a legalistic tone in Puritanism was doubtless the Calvinist stress on a single covenant in Scripture…which elevated the Old Testament to a position of great prominence in Puritan theology. Old Testament laws were indiscriminately applied to New Testament situations (cf. Earle's detailed work, *The Sabbath in Puritan New England*)…Puritan Calvinist preoccupation with the history of salvation in the Old Testament gave a special cast to the New England colonists' western dream… consistent with their Old Testament interests, they went on to identify themselves with Israel, reading their own history as the story of a new Chosen People (*The Shaping of America* [Bethany, 1976]. pp. 44–45).

The Covenant of Grace and "Conditions"

There were varying ideas among covenant theologians as to whether the covenant of grace was "conditional" (upon faith and repentance) or "unconditional" (cf. Shantz, pp. 3-4). Here, I simply wish to point out my judgment that in Puritanism the emphasis came to fall on the "conditions" (cf. William K. B. Stoever, '*A Faire and Easie Way to Heaven*'— *Covenant Theology and Antinomianism in Early Massachusetts* [Wesleyan Univ. Press. 1978], "The Conditionality of the

Covenant of Grace," p. 97ff.; R. T. Kendall. "Assurance and Sanctification" [taped message]; and Norman Pettit, *The Heart Prepared* [Yale Univ. Press, 1966]). The idea of "entering into covenant" with God was accompanied by such ideas as putting one-self in the "way of grace," the "probability" of success in conversion with the use of the "means of grace," and "striving against our corruption" while seeking our salvation (cf. Stoever, pp. 105-106).

Iain Murray insists that in all of this the Puritans were not "reviving the idea of human ability in salvation" ("Thomas Hooker and the Doctrine of Conversion (3)," *Banner of Truth*, Feb., 1980, p. 17). The Puritans clearly intended to maintain human inability in salvation, but their emphasis on "means" and "striving" also intended and communicated *more* than just the duty of people to believe the gospel.

Consider the following remarks by Josph Alleine, John Flavel and George Whitefield. Judge for yourself whether or not the effects of such teaching would open the door wide for misunderstanding and confusion concerning the place of human activity in the salvation process.

Joseph Alleine

"Being thus prepared, on some convenient time set apart for the purpose, enter upon the work, and solemnly, as in the presence of the Lord, fall down on your knees and spreading forth your hands towards heaven open your heart to the Lord in these, or the like words: [a prayer three pages long follows]…This covenant I advise you to make, not only in heart, but in word; not only in word, but in writing; and that you would with all possible reverence spread the writing before the Lord, as if you *would present it to Him as your Act and Deed.* And when you have done this, set your hand to it and sign it. Keep it as a memorial of the solemn transactions that have passed between God and you, that you may *have recourse to it in doubts and temptations*" (*Alarm To The Unconverted* [1671; Banner of Truth 1967] pp. 117, 120).

John Flavel

"Objection: But you have told us that no sinner can open his own heart, nor bow his own will to Christ? Answer: True, he cannot convert himself, but he may do many things in order to it, and which have a tendency to it, which he does not do…If it be not in your power to open your heart to Christ, it is in your power to forbear the external acts of sin, which set your heart the more against Christ…Objection: [After all our striving] we may be Christless and hopeless when all is done. Answer: But yet remember, God may bless these weak endeavours, and give you his Almighty Spirit with them: nay, it is *highly probable that he will do so; and is a strong probability nothing with you?*" (*Christ Knocking At The Door of Sinners Hearts,* pp. 58, 60).

George Whitefield

"Wait therefore at Wisdom's gates. The bare probability of having a door of mercy opened, is enough to keep you striving…You know not but you may be in the number of those few, and that your striving may be the means which God intends to bless, to give you an entrance in… For though after you have done all that you can, God may justly cut you off. Yet never was a single person damned who did all that he could" (*Memoirs of George Whitefield.* John Gillies [1834], sermon on John 16:8, p. 418).

The elements of Alleine's remarks ("sinner's prayer," signing a document, and looking to that document in times of doubt) parallel contemporary Evangelicalism's shallow methods, often castigated by the Calvinists. Yet we are told in the prefatory remarks to *Alarm* that "here, we have no hesitation in saying, are the principles which must be present in any true presentation of the Gospel." I believe contemporary believers need to read such Puritan material with great discernment.

The Covenant of Grace and Law

The doctrine of the covenant also served to emphasize "the importance of the Decalogue [Ten Commandments] for the Christian life" (De Jong. p.22). According to covenant theology, the "substance" of the Decalogue was present from Adam onwards. Thus, in this system, "the law from the beginning was a means of grace" (E. Kevan. *The Law of God in Christian Experience—Bible Readings Given at the Keswick Conference*, July 1955 [London 1955]. p. 48).

I suggest that this approach fails to do justice to the centrality of Christ in ethics (cf. "'This Is My Beloved Son…Hear Him'" *BRR*, 1978, 7:4, pp. 15-52). At this point, I wish to make several pointed observations about covenant theology's view of law in Christian experience.

First, Witsius made the following remarks about the Ten Commandments: "all prescription of duty belongs to the law…[in the teaching of Christ and the apostles] there is a certain mixture of various doctrines…each of which ought to be reduced to their proper heads, so that the promises of grace might be referred to the gospel, all injunctions of duty…to the law" (pp. 407, 411). Does this hard and fast distinction reflect sensitivity to the *N.T. ethical perspective?* Is it not the case that in the N.T. duties are pressed upon believers because of their relationship *to the grace of Christ in the Gospel?* (Cf. my "Believer's Rule of Life." *BRR*. 1979, 8:4, p. 16). "Love one another, *even as I have loved you*," is the starting point of Christian ethics. "Under grace," *duty flows out of union with Christ.*

In Witsius' scheme, the gospel is said not to prescribe duty, *only* the law is granted this function. But how contrary this is to N.T. teaching (cf. C.H. Dodd. *Gospel and Law* [New York,1951]; "Principles and Motives of Christian Ethics in the New Testament." pp. 25-45)!

Because everything is subsumed under the one covenant of grace, covenant theology has not done justice to the new demand that obtains with the coming of Christ. The command to love is *old*; the command to love as it is connected to the decisive redemptive event of the cross is *new* (John 13:34-35; 15:12-13).

Patrick Fairbairn said that the Law is the "special instrument…for keeping alive in men's souls a sense of duty" (*Revelation of Law in Scripture*, p. 289). Will such a statement stand the test of N.T. perspectives? Ethics in covenant theology has been oriented around Moses, not Christ.

Secondly, covenant theology puts the believer in a tension of being both "under law" and "not under law." Samuel Bolton put it like this:

> The law sends us to the Gospel that we may be justified, and the Gospel sends us to the law again to inquire what is our duty as those who are justified…It is a hard lesson to live above the law, and yet walk according to the law… To walk in the law in respect of duty, but to live above it in respect of comfort (*True Bounds of Christian Freedom*, pp. 71, 219, 220).

Where does the N.T. teach all of this?

I submit that (1) this places Christians in a position God has never intended for them: and (2) that this is contrary to the N.T. teaching on sanctification. On the one hand, covenant theology tells us that the law promotes transgressions, stirs up sin, brings death, and cannot be the means of sanctification (Kevan, pp. 30, 38, 49, 77). Yet, on the other hand, we are told that "grace is more commanding than law." They say "that it is a mark of spiritual infancy...to be under the law," but then say that in sanctification we are left "within the law as a rule of life" (Kevan. pp. 66, 59, 68).

Our approach to the law must be *through Christ*. "Moses wrote of Me," Jesus said. Perhaps the following diagram will help illustrate my point:

OLD EXODUS	NEW EXODUS
(Moses, mediator)	(Christ, Mediator)
Redemptive Event:	**Redemptive Event:**
"I have brought you out [of Egypt]"	"I have loved you" [in the cross]
(Exodus 20:2)	(John 15:12–15)
Moral Demand:	**Moral Demand:**
"no other gods"	"love one another"
"honor your father/mother"	"children obey your parents *in the Lord*, honor your father/mother"

The N.T. uses the O.T. freely (2.Tim. 3:16). But the O.T. is not viewed in isolation from the consummation of redemptive history in the New Covenant (cf. "Believer's Rule of Life." p. 19). When Christ said, "if you love me keep my commandments" (John 14:15), He did not mean, "keep all the old covenant commandments." He meant that our attention was to be fixed on *His* commandments (cf. D.M. Canright, "What Law Are Christians Under?" *BRR*, 9:1, 1980, pp. 11-13; cf. Walter Chantry, *Today's Gospel: Authentic or Synthetic?*, pp. 40-41, where he equates Christ's commandments with the Ten Commandments). In our sanctification, we are "in-law to Christ" (1 Cor. 9:21), and are enabled to "fully fulfil (*anaplerosete*) the law of Christ" (Gal. 6:2).

Thirdly, covenant theology allows for no other means of conviction than the Ten Commandments. "It is the law that brings conviction of sin" (Kevan, p. 40). "Our Saviour used the law as a primary tool of evangelism. He knew that preaching the Ten Commandments was the *only way* to teach a sinner his guilt and thereby stir within him a desire for God's grace" (Walter Chantry, *Today's Gospel*, p. 39; emphasis mine). We have already seen that covenant theology rules out the gospel's ability to press duty; now we see that the gospel is denied the power to produce conviction. Covenant theology dogmatically asserts that *law must be preached before the gospel* (cf. Charles Bridges, *The Christian Ministry*, pp. 222-238).

But we must ask some questions. Are the Ten Commandments the "only way" to teach sinners their guilt? Apparently not, for Paul specifically said that when he was among Gentiles his evangelistic method was "without law" (1 Cor. 9:21). He nowhere used the Ten Commandments with Gentiles to convict them of sin. There is no evidence of this in the brief talks addressed to Gentiles that are recorded in Acts 14:15-17 and 17:23-31. Rather, as can be seen in Rom. 1, his starting point was *general revelation*, the creation. Furthermore, even the use of the O.T. *special revelation* in

Acts does not reveal the use of the Ten Commandments to drive men to Christ. Rather, *Christ* in all of His functions is proclaimed (Acts 17:2-3; 26:22-23).

If "law preaching" is *essential*, as the Puritans asserted it was, why do we not find any examples of this method in Acts? Would we not expect something so allegedly crucial to be *clearly* revealed in apostolic preaching? But as F.F. Bruce observes, "there is no evidence that Paul ever used the law in this way" (*Paul: Apostle of the Heart Set Free*, p. 192).

Does the N.T. teach that the law is the *only* medium of sin-conviction?

John 16:8-11 is admittedly the most important passage concerning Holy Spirit conviction. George Smeaton said of it: "the most conclusive passage on the Spirit's work in connection with conversion in the whole compass of Scripture." After studying this passage extensively, I can see nowhere the teaching that the Spirit will take law-preaching and drive men to Christ. I have found no commentator who finds the exclusive use of the law by the Spirit in this text. Rather, as Leon Morris notes: "it should not be overlooked that all three aspects of the work of the Holy Spirit dealt with in these verses are interpreted Christologically. Sin, righteousness and judgment are all to be understood because of the way they relate to Christ" (*Commentary on John*, p.699). Thus James Buchanan said about this passage in his book on the Holy Spirit: "it may be safely affirmed that it is by the Spirit's witness to Christ that he is *first* brought to see the magnitude of his guilt…Christ's exaltation…is *sufficient*…to carry home conviction of sin."

Walter Chantry says: "until this moralist [the rich young ruler] could see his sin in the light of God's law, he was unprepared for the Gospel...[When pulpits proclaim the law] you also discover churches with convicted sinners prepared to hear the way of salvation" (*Today's Gospel*, pp. 38-46). Does the N.T. divide sinners into categories of "prepared" and "unprepared" with reference to hearing the gospel?

Was the Philippian jailor "prepared" for the imperative to believe in Christ by Ten Commandment preaching? Who determines when a man is "sufficiently" convicted by the law so as to be "fit" for advancing on to the gospel? Where in the N.T is Ten Commandment preaching presented as a *necessary* prerequisite which "prepares" men for the "message of salvation"?

I believe that the dogmatism regarding "law preaching" must be re-examined in the light of Scripture. Binding the consciences of Bible-teachers (who wish to be faithful in their ministries) and sinners (who may sit under the Word) to the absolute necessity of Ten Commandment preaching elicits a type of bondage, because such a method is out of line with the N.T. story.

The Puritans took this matter of "law preaching" very seriously, as the following quote from John Owen demonstrates:

What is necessary to be found in us antecedaneously to our believing unto the justification of life?...There is supposed in whom this faith is wrought...the work of the law in conviction of sin...that which any man hath first to deal withal...is the law...Without this the gospel cannot be understood, nor the grace of it duly valued...the faith which we treat of being evangelical...cannot be acted by us, but on a supposition of the work and effect of the law...And that faith which hath not respect hereunto, we absolutely deny to be that faith whereby we are justified, Gal. 3:22-24; Rom. 10:4 (*Justification*, pp. 74-76).

Will the N.T. sustain such a strict opinion? In light of the truth claims made by Owen, we need to be clear on this matter. Let's examine several crucial texts.

Galatians 3:19-20

Verse 20 has often been used to show that the Ten Commandments must be preached to convict of sin: "God's law is an *essential* ingredient of gospel preaching, for 'by the law is the knowledge of sin'" (Chantry, p. 36). Historically, the "law" in 3:20b has been equated with the Ten Commandments. But there is nothing in the context to warrant this conclusion. In verse 9 Paul states that all humans are "under sin." He proves this by quoting from the "law." Here he has in view *the entire* O.T. (John Murray. *Romans*. Vol. 1, pp. 240, 105). The translation "under law" in v. 19 is incorrect. The Greek is *en nomos* ("in the law"), not *hupo nomos* ("under the law"). Whatever the O.T. says, it says to those described *in* it, namely Jews and Gentiles (Murray, p. 106). Thus, while the Ten Commandments are a part of the O.T., the "law" in 3:20b certainly cannot be *equated* with the Ten, and contextually it refers to *the whole Old Testament*. If anyone reads Genesis through Malachi, he will come to a full knowledge of sin—the sin of Adam, the sin that brought the flood, the sin that brought fire upon Sodom, the sin that caused Israel to be cast out of the land, etc.…*and thereby come to a knowledge of their sinfulness*.

Galatians 3:21

This is a very significant verse, for it is a transition from the proven unrighteousness of humans to the revealed righteousness of God. In this verse, I believe we have an assertion of both the *discontinuity* and *continuity* of the Old and New Covenants (cf. Murray. *Romans*. Vol.1 p. 109). The *discontinuity* is revealed in the phrase, "without law a righteousness of God has been manifested." "Righteousness" cannot come by the law. Therefore, the gospel righteousness of God has come apart from the law, that is, "'in a sphere different from that in which the law says, 'do this and live'"' (*Wuest's Word Studies, Romans*. p. 57).

John Brown says: "without law" means that this righteousness "stands apart from law; it is founded upon other principles: it is characterized by different qualities" (*Commentary on Romans, ad.* 3:21). The "now" of 3:21, says John Murray, should not "be deprived of its temporal force" (*Romans*. Vol.1, p. 108). "When Paul says 'without the law' the absoluteness of this negative must not be toned down" (*Ibid.*, p. 109). Thus, Murray continues, "the emphasis falls upon the manifestation without law rather than upon the fact that it is righteousness without law" (*Ibid.*, p. 110).

In this Messianic age, then, a righteousness has been manifested which is "apart from the law." It is founded, not on the principle "do this and live," but "on the law of faith" (3:27). This, then, is the essence of what Paul means in Gal. 3:12 when he says that the law "is not of faith." Because this righteousness is *"without law," it is for Jews and Gentiles* (3:22-23). Paul shows in 4:10 that righteousness by faith came to Abraham "without law"—and in his case, *prior* to the law.

The *continuity* in 3:21 is seen in the fact that this righteousness is witnessed to in the O.T. Habakkuk 2:4, for example, often quoted in the N.T., teaches justification by faith. While the law, contemplated as a legal covenant, was "not of faith," the O.T. documents taught righteousness by faith (Gal. 3:11-12). The gospel, then, was manifested in history apart from law, but was foretold in the law (Gal. 3:8).

The history of covenant theology shows a tendency to overplay *continuity,* and not to do justice to the revealed *discontinuity* of the two covenants. Discontinuity is virtually ruled out as a possibility when *all* covenants are viewed as administrations of one covenant of grace.

Dispensationalists, on the other hand, have ruled out the possibility of *continuity* by teaching that the O.T. is "silent" about this present "intercalation" age. We must do full justice to *all* that is revealed in Rom. 3:21.

Romans 3:31

Historically, covenant theology has seen this text as establishing the abiding validity of the "moral law" under the gospel. Charles Hodge is representative of this when he says concerning this text, "no moral obligation is weakened" (*Commentary on Romans, ad.* 3:31). However, it appears that Paul's point here, and in the preceding and following context, is *to validate the fact that his teaching is not contrary to the Old Testament.*

In Romans 3:27, Paul uses the phrase "law of faith" as opposed to salvation by works. Some might suppose that this invalidates the O.T. Thus in 3:31, he indicates that his gospel upholds the law, for righteousness by faith was "witnessed by the law and prophets" (3:21). F.F. Bruce summarizes the teaching of 3:31 and the context by saying:

> "do we then overthrow the law by this faith?"…"By no means! On the contrary, we uphold the law." In the immediate context, in which Paul goes on to expound the narrative of Abraham's faith which was reckoned to

him for righteousness (4:1-25), it might appear that the law which is upheld by the gospel of justification by faith is the Torah in the wider sense—the Pentateuch, and more particularly the Genesis account of Abraham. That is so, but Paul goes on farther to show that the law in its stricter sense, as the embodiment of God's will, is upheld and fulfilled more adequately in the age of faith than was possible "before faith came," when law kept the people "under restraint" (Gal. 3:23). Only in an atmosphere of spiritual liberty can God's will be properly obeyed and his law upheld (*Heart Set Free*, p. 201).

In summarizing this Romans context, I believe the remarks of Geerhardus Vos are appropriate and insightful:

> It is evident that there are two distinct points of view from which the content of the old dispensation can be regarded. When considered in comparison with the final unfolding and rearranged structure of the N.T., negative judgments are in place. When, on the other hand, the O.T. is taken as an entirety by itself and rounded off provisionally in itself, and looked at, as it were, with the eyes of the O.T. itself, we find it necessary to take into account the positive elements by which it is prefigured and anticipated typically in the N.T. (*Biblical Theology*, p. 144).

Galatians 3:1-6:2

In this context, it appears to me that we must remember that Paul is dealing with people who have been urged to come *under Moses*. This makes his appeal to the *law of Christ* in 6:2 take on an increased significance.

Gal. 3:1-5—Paul confronts the Galatians with the original way in which they came to Christ. The answer to his question is obvious: they came to Christ through *faith*, not through *the law*. Covenant theology has argued, and not without textual foundation (Gal. 5:4), that the issue here is not *sanctification*, but *justification*. Their position, of course, avers that the Christian is not under the law for justification, but that he is under the law in sanctification. However, it is impossible to separate the *way* of justification and sanctification in the N.T. If we are justified *by faith*, so we are sanctified *by faith*—the just shall live by faith in all of their days (cf. H. Bavinck. *Our Reasonable Faith* [Baker, 1978], p. 480). If justification does not come by the law, then to Paul, neither does sanctification: "if you are led by the Spirit, you are not under the law" (Gal. 5:18; cf. Rom. 6:14). The gospel brings justification, sanctification, and all blessings in Christ. Many Galatians were trying to *maintain their standing before God* with the law, and Paul tells them it just will not work (cf. Thom. Smith. "Have You Fallen From Grace?", *Free Grace Herald*, May, 1979).

Gal. 3:17-29—Paul here shows that blessing comes via the Abrahamic promise. Abraham stands as our reference point in the history of redemption. He was justified by faith *prior* to his own circumcision, and 430 years *prior* to the law. Abraham was essentially a heathen when justified—he was without law and uncircumcised. Thus for believers to come under the Mosaic covenant is retrogressive and dangerous.

For Paul there is obviously some tremendously significant difference between the Abrahamic-promise and Mosaic-law covenants. The one was a *unilateral* declaration of God's purpose in Christ (3:16-17: cf. Gen. 15:17-18). The other was *bi-lateral*, and involved the consent of the people (Exod. 19:8; 24:7). The Abrahamic covenant was incapable of being forfeited; the Mosaic covenant was conditioned upon obedience, and indeed was "broken" (Jer. 31:32). However, in covenant theology, the Mosaic covenant is transformed into a "fresh administration of the covenant of grace" (cf. 7:3), and asserted to be *the same in substance as the covenant with Abraham*. Frankly, in this regard, there is no place in covenant theology for Paul's line of reasoning in Gal. 3:17-29. Redemptive history is levelled, with the result that *all* covenants are the same.

Further, covenant theology has historically viewed this context with reference to *effectual calling*, and not with reference to *salvation history*. We must understand the apostle's perspective in this context.

Gal. 3:24—The "to bring us" is *in italics* in the King James Version. These words are not in the Greek text. It should read, "the law was our schoolmaster unto [or *until*] Christ." The "to bring us" rendering makes it appear that Paul has in view our *personal calling* into salvation. Gal. 3:24, based on this idea, has been used to teach that in the process of salvation, people *must first* be convicted by the Ten Commandments, and *then* are driven to Christ. For example, Archbishop Usher said, "First, the *covenant of the law is urged*, to make sin, and the punishment thereof known…*After this preparation, the promises of God are propounded*" (quoted by Bridges. *Christian Ministry*, pp. 233-324). Walter Chantry states that gospel preachers must "exposit the Ten Commandments until men are slain thereby (Rom. 7:11). When you see that men have been wounded by the law, then it is time to pour in the balm of Gospel oil. It is the sharp needle of the law that makes way for the scarlet thread of the Gospel" (*Today's Gospel*, p. 43). But, clearly, this is not what Paul is teaching in Gal. 3:24. Rather he is showing the *advance of history* from the Abrahamic covenant to the Mosaic covenant, to the coming of Christ. He does this to show that salvation is of *faith*, not *of law* (3:18), and that salvation is connected with *promise*, not *law* (3:17).

Notice the following *historical* terminology in this context: "430 years *after*...[the law] was *added*...*till* the seed should come...*before* faith came, we [Jews] were kept under the law, shut up to the faith which should *afterwards* be revealed...the law was our schoolmaster *until* Christ...But after that faith is come, we are no longer under a schoolmaster...*until the time* appointed of the father...the *fullness of time was come.*" Ernest DeWitt Burton said concerning Gal. 3:24:

> Nor is the reference to the individual experience under the law as bringing men individually to faith in Christ. For the context makes it clear that the apostle is speaking, rather, of the historic succession of one period of revelation upon another and the displacement of the law by Christ. (*Galatians*. p. 200).

This text, probably more than any other, has been used to prove that law *must* be preached before gospel. In fact, the Puritans built a whole theology of "law-preaching" on this text. But this is a misunderstanding of the mind of the Spirit. That the Ten Commandments *must* convict Jews and Gentiles *prior* to gospel preaching is the last thing in Paul's mind *in this* text. If the Galatians had been so driven to the gospel by the law in the beginning, would not his point that they are not "made perfect" through the law *after* salvation lose its punch?

Gal. 4:10-11.15—I would just point out here that we need to mark well the danger of coming "under law" (cf. 5:18). There is something to be afraid of when we go one-on-one with the law (cf. Anthony Hoekema, *The Christian Looks At*

Himself, "Romans Seven," *BRR,* Autumn, 1980). The "sense of blessing" the gospel brings with it simply cannot be maintained when a person is "under law." Paul therefore, feared for people when they lost sight of their status in Christ as "under grace" (Rom. 6:14). Because covenant theology is so old covenant oriented, as I believe its history amply demonstrates, and makes no qualms about keeping the Christian "under the conduct of Moses" (Bolton, p. 76), inherent dangers are built into the system. The Christian is asked to learn the "hard lesson" (rather, "impossible") of stopping his ears to the curses of the law with reference to justification, but opening his ears to that same law for sanctification. Thus in order to maintain this system, Abraham is put under the yoke of the law, and the Mosaic covenant is said to be the same as the Abrahamic!

Gal. 6:2—The false teachers in Galatia were imposing dangerous burdens on the brethren. Paul exhorts them, therefore, to turn away from these burdens, and to rather give themselves to the bearing of one another's burdens. In this way they will fully fulfil the "law of Christ."

The Jewish people were weighed down with many burdens imposed by the Pharisees: "they tie up heavy loads and put them on peoples' shoulders" (Matt. 23:4); "you load people down with burdens they can hardly carry" (Luke 11:46). Secondly, there was a burden of the Mosaic economy itself: "a yoke that neither we nor our fathers have been able to bear" (Acts 15:10). It is in the light of these *burdens* that we must understand the invitations of Christ in Matt. 11:28. "come to Me, all you who are weary and burdened, and I will give you rest [Sabbath]."

In Galatia, then, the Judaizers were putting the believers under such burdens again. Paul challenges them to bear one another's burdens, and in this way they will fulfil Christ's law. Thus, to paraphrase, Paul is saying: "I would have you to bear, not the burden of the Mosaic law (which none can bear), but bear *one another's burdens* and thereby fulfill *Christ's law.*" What does Paul mean by "the law of Christ"? It is the "new commandment" *to love one another* (John 13:34-35; 15:12-13). I think John Brown's words are most instructive here:

> "The law" here [5:14] plainly does not signify the Mosaic law, but the law by which Christians are bound to regulate themselves, for, as the apostle elsewhere says, though completely free from the obligation of the Mosaic law, they are "not without law to God, but in-law to Christ"… There seems to be a tacit contrast in [6:2] between the law of Moses and the law of Christ." It is as if the apostle had said, "This bearing one another's burdens is a far better thing than those external observations which your new teachers are so anxious to impose upon you. To be sure, it is not like them, a keeping of the law of Moses, but infinitely better, it is a fulfilling of the law of Christ—the law of love. (*Galatians*, pp. 287, 326).

In light of the fact that in his Galatian Epistle Paul has in view the imposition of the Mosaic system on believers, his focus on the "law of Christ" is all the more significant. It indicates where our attention is to be directed in this age: to the words of the Prophet in Whom God has spoken in these last days (Acts 3:22-23; Matt. 7:24; 17:5). ■

Crucial Questions to Consider Before the Lord's Word, In Light of the Presuppositions Examined:

1. Does the Bible teach that God has two separate purposes, an earthly one for Israel and a heavenly one for the church?

2. In the final analysis, is Dispensationalism *Christ*-centered or *Israel-* centered?

3. Does the Bible teach that the "covenant of works/covenant of grace" are the two "primary" covenants in Scripture?

4. Is "covenant" a specifically *historical* term? Does a covenant have an historical moment when it is "cut"?

5. Is it *Scriptural* to apply "covenant" terminology to the pre-temporal Trinitarian counsel?

6. Does the Bible teach that the "Old Covenant" is the entire period from the Adam/Eve's fall to Christ's coming?

7. Does the Bible teach that there is a "covenant of grace" *above history*, inaugurated *after* the fall, which is then mirrored in the subsequent *historical* covenants?

8. Covenant theologians constantly use the phrase, "the covenant," in their writings (cf. Errol Hulse, *Reformation Today*, #53, p.6). What "covenant" is in view? Where is *this* "covenant" revealed in Scripture, and where was it "cut" in history?

9. Does the status of being "under law" accurately describe the pre-fall condition of Adam?

10. Where does the N.T. *require* that the Ten Commandments be preached *before* the gospel?

11. Where does the N.T. describe the Christian as facing the "hard lesson" of being "not under the law" in justification, yet being "under the law" to grow in grace?

12. Is the New Covenant based on the same "do this and live" principle as the Old Covenant?

A Generalized Comparison of Dispensationalism and Covenant Theology

DISPENSATIONALISM	COVENANT THEOLOGY
Two separate purposes	One covenant of grace
Israel: Future	Israel: Present
Earthly purpose	Political model
Law/Grace opposed	Law/Grace fused together
Law postponed to future	Law carried over into the New Covenant
Redemptive History	**Redemptive History**
Chopped up	Flattened
Assume literalism	Assume one covenant
Avoid NT use of OT	Avoid historical covenants
Read the OT without the NT	Read the NT into the OT
Eschatological rigidity	Eschatological liberty
(*only* dispensational Premillennialism tolerated)	(historic pre-mill, a-mill, and post-mill allowed)

THE NEW EXODUS / THE NEW COMMANDMENT / THE NEW SPIRIT: TOWARD A CHRIST-CENTERED LIFE

JON ZENS, 1979

In 1979, Steve Carpenter invited me to come and speak to a fellowship in Houston, Texas, on the pre-eminence of Christ. My presentations on some crucial matters related to the "new" that came in Jesus generated a huge amount of discussion among the saints. Before I came, one brother announced he would not come to the meetings because he viewed me as a heretic. He ended up coming to the last session on Sunday, and was struck with what he heard. A group of us had breakfast on Monday morning, and he came. He sat next to me. I ended up drawing some comparisons and diagrams on a place setting. His eyes were opened to the fact that the Bible was about Christ, not Moses, and as we parted he gave me a hug of thanks.

THE NEW EXODUS

A strong case can be made that often in the history of theology Christ has played second fiddle to the law.[1] One central reason why this has been the case flows out of the old covenant orientation that has characterized theological enterprise since Constantine made Christianity the official religion of the Roman Empire around 325 A.D. The rationale for a state-church could not be found in the New Testament. The Old Testament, however, did provide a model where religion and government were intertwined under the Mosaic economy. The strong influence of this model can be seen in the histories of both England and America.[2] As a result, most systems of theology have paid little attention to the implications of Christ's coming and His inauguration of a New Covenant. They have been rooted more in Moses' thunderings than in Christ's grace.

This approach misuses the Old Testament text and the types and shadows embedded in Israel's history and institutions. Christ saw the Old Testament as focused on His person and His mission (Luke 24:27, 44-45), not as a foundation for civil government among Gentile nations. Colossians 2:17 states that Christ is the substance (reality) of the types and shadows of the old covenant administration. It seems to me that by examining the Exodus theme we can see Israel's ancient deliverance out of Egypt as a type which was fulfilled in the fullness of time by Jesus' death, burial, and resurrection.[3] It is only upon the foundation of a New Exodus that a truly New Covenant theology can emerge.

Our examination will focus on Luke 9:28-36, an awesome account of our Lord's transfiguration. We will look at

SEARCHING TOGETHER | FALL-WINTER 2018

the general context of the transfiguration in light of John 1:14-18, and then the specific context in Luke 9:18-27 (and the parallel passage, Matt. 17:13-28).

John 1:14-18

The Word that was God, was with God in the beginning, and through whom all things were created, was made flesh in the fullness of time (v.14). John indicates that there was a striking characteristic about this Word: He was "full of grace and truth" (v.14). It is correct to say that Jesus Christ was the incarnation of grace and truth. It is from this inestimable fullness that His disciples received "grace upon grace" *(charin anti charitos,* v.16). This is a difficult phrase to capture in English, but it conveys the image of waves incessantly coming upon a shore—wave upon wave. He who is Himself "grace and truth" communicates to His people wave upon wave of grace in order that they may live to His glory in this present evil age.

On the heels of this "grace upon grace" perspective, John then sets forth a very significant contrast. He asserts, "For the law was given through Moses; grace and truth were realized through Jesus Christ"(v.17). He points out here that an old covenant administration of law has been eclipsed now by a New Covenant economy of grace and truth. The law was mediated (Gal. 3:19). You cannot say that "Moses is the law." On the other hand, the New Covenant has a peculiar directness about it. You can say that Jesus Christ is grace and truth, and His administration is effective, unlike the law, in bringing the reign of righteousness (Rom. 8:1-3).

It is against this backdrop that we must approach the events that took place in our Lord's transfiguration. When

Moses and Elijah left the scene and the three disciples saw "Jesus only," God wished to underscore the fact that the old covenant and its institutions were finished, and in the gospel age people must listen to the Beloved Son who sealed the New Covenant with His blood.

Luke 9:18-27 (Matthew 17:13-28)

An encounter of the Lord with His disciples about a week before the transfiguration reveals five issues that emerged in the specific context.

Confession. Sufficient time with the Lord having elapsed, Jesus asks them, "Who do you say that I am?" They confess that He is the Christ, the Son of the Living God. The *ekklesia* (congregation) Christ purposes to build consists of those who personally confess Jesus Christ as Lord. Under the old covenant physical birth constituted one a member of the community. Under the New Covenant participation is not defined by human parentage, but only by the Father's action of revealing Christ to His elect people.

Commission. To the people who confess His name for salvation, Christ gives the keys of the kingdom. These keys function as His assemblies carry out God's will on earth (Matt. 18:17-18). Just as the Old Testament documents defined covenant life for Israel, so the New Testament writings give apostolic direction for life under the New Covenant.

Crucifixion. In the setting of the disciples' confession of their Lord, from this point on He began to show them that He had to be crucified and raised the third day. The idea of a suffering Christ was absolutely foreign to Jewish expectations regarding the Messiah. It is not surprising, therefore, that Peter took issue with Jesus' announcement and said, "Let it never be, Lord! This will never happen to you." Jesus assigned those sentiments to Satan, indicating that the course of suffering (with resulting glory) was inevitable in God's eternal purpose for His Son.

Commitment. In light of His own imminent encounter with an ignominious cross, Jesus confronted the disciples with the reality that cross-bearing will be an integral part of their lives under the New Covenant.

Coming. The return of Jesus Christ in glory will result in life and immortality for those who lost their lives for Him on earth, and judgment for those who lived selfishly and gained all that the world had to offer.

The Transfiguration: Moses and Elijah discuss Christ's 'Exodus' (Luke 9:28-36; Matt. 17:1-9; Mark 9:2-9)

The Climb. About a week after the sayings in the immediate context, Jesus took Peter and John and "brought them up to a high mountain by themselves." Some fanciful interpretations have arisen in connection with this passage. Paul VanGorder of the Radio Bible Class posits that the "six days" correspond to six past dispensations (as popularized in the *Scofield Bible* notes), and the transfiguration of Jesus symbolizes the glory of Christ in the seventh and final dispensation, the Millennium!

In this event on a mountain we have, as J.A. Alexander suggests, "a crisis in the history of redemption."[4] Alfred Edersheim designates the transfiguration as one of "the most solemn turning-points" of history.[5]

The Change. Before the three chosen disciples Jesus underwent a 'metamorphosis,' a transfiguration in which "His face shone like the sun, and his garments became as white as light." Is it any wonder that Peter refers to this awesome event etched in his memory in 2 Peter 1:16-18?

> We did not follow cleverly invented stories when we told you about the power and coming of our Lord Jesus Christ, but we were eyewitnesses of His majesty. For He received honor and glory from God the Father when the voice came to Him from the Majestic Glory saying: "This is my Son, whom I love; with Him I am well pleased." We ourselves heard this voice that came from the mountain when we were with Him on the sacred mountain.

The Conversation. As if the startling metamorphosis of Jesus was not enough, "behold, Moses and Elijah appeared to them, talking with Him." These two figures were "the great pillars and representatives of the Old Testament dispensation."[6] Moses and Elijah were the greatest names on Israel's roll of honor."[7] Moses led Israel out of Egypt in the Red Sea exodus. In connection with his departure from Elisha, Elijah was also involved in an exodus:

> And Elijah took his mantle and folded it together and struck the waters, and they were divided here and there, so that the two of them crossed over on dry ground (2 Kings 2:1-14).

What was the topic of conversation between Christ, Moses and Elijah? Luke 9:31 reports that they "were speaking of His departure [Greek, *exodus*] which He was about to accomplish at Jerusalem." The *exodus*, or departure, of Christ consisted of His death, burial resurrection and ascension to God's right hand.

In his message at Pisidian Antioch, Paul referred to the incarnation of Jesus as his *eisodos*, literally, an incoming (Acts 13:24). In Luke 9:31 Jesus leaving the earth is called an *exodus*, a departure. The big picture can be seen in the parallels between the Red Sea exodus and the Jerusalem exodus. In the ancient exodus from Egypt God took His people out of the land of bondage, they took the spoils with them, experienced redemption by crossing on dry land, and ultimately entered into the promised land. In the New Exodus, Christ by His redemptive work takes His people out of the bondage of sin, as the ascended Lord of Glory pours out gifts upon His people (Eph. 4:6-7) and ultimately brings them into the promised "Sabbath rest" (Heb. 4:9).

Just as the old exodus resulted in the separation of a covenant nation to God, so the New Exodus resulted in a "new creation," the body of Christ (Acts 20:28). After Israel was set apart from the rest of the nations by God's saving action (Exodus 2:2), He gave them "the law" through Moses. The Red Sea exodus constituted the foundation for Israel's obedience. "I stretched out my saving arm on your behalf…therefore, you must live in the following manner." Likewise, the New Exodus in Christ forms the basis for life under the New Covenant. 1 John 3:15 crystallizes this vital perspective: "He laid down His life for us [redemptive act]; and we ought to lay down our lives for the brethren [loving obedience]." In the context of His impending death, His *exodus*, Jesus gave us a "new commandment, to love one another, as I have loved you [at Calvary]" (John 13:34). As the exodus from Egypt was the basis for Israel's covenant life, so Christ's New Exodus not only saved His people, but also commanded them how to live. "If God so loved us [by sending His Son], we ought also to love one another" (1 John 4:11).

The Confusion. As could be expected, seeing Christ, Moses and Elijah speaking to each other while shrouded in glory was a terrifying experience. It is not surprising, therefore, that Peter "did not know what to answer." Silence would have been entirely appropriate, but impetuous Peter hastily suggested, "Rabbi, it is good for us to be here; and let us make three tabernacles, one for You, one for Moses, and one for Elijah." The next event made any reply to Peter unnecessary.

The Cloud. "While Peter was still speaking, behold, a bright cloud overshadowed them." This occurrence is reminiscent of the Shekinah glory that appeared in various times in Israel's history. But now the glory of God centers upon His only Son, Who is the brightness of His glory.

The Command. From the midst of this glorious cloud came the voice of God. The words that God now sends forth confirm the truth of Hebrews 1:1-2.

> God, after He spoke long ago to the fathers in the prophets [like Moses and Elijah] in many portions and in many ways, in these last days has spoken to us in a Son, whom he appointed heir of all things, through whom also He made the world.

Parallel to the words uttered when Jesus was baptized (Matt. 3:17), Peter, James and John heard from the awesome cloud, "This is my beloved Son, with whom I am well-pleased; hear Him!"

The voice of God cited the crucial words from Moses' writings in Deut. 18:15,18, "Hear Him!" This clearly indicates the superiority and finality of the Father speaking in His Son. There can be no question that the emphasis of this command falls specifically on the words of the Son. John Gill notes that "Hear Him" points to Christ "as being the Prophet who is to be heard and He only; not Moses...not Elijah...

but one greater than them all, hear Him always and in all things." Matthew Poole rightly observes in commenting on Matthew 17:5:

> "Hear Him"—which words establish Christ as the only Doctor and Teacher of His church, the only one to whom [God] had entrusted to deliver His truths and will to His people, the only one to whom Christians are to hearken… And this command from God to us to hear Christ lets us see the audacity of those who take upon them to impose upon Christians what Christ never spoke.

The Comfort. "And when the disciples heard this, they fell on their faces and were much afraid." No wonder! They had just heard the Lord God speak from the Shekinah glory giving full approbation to Jesus Christ. In full sympathy with what the disciples had just experienced. Jesus mercifully comforts them by coming to them, touching them, and saying, "Arise and do not be afraid."

The Climax. All that had transpired on the mountain that day comes to an unequivocal climax when they "lifted up their eyes and saw no one, except Jesus Himself alone" (Matt. 17:8). "And all at once they looked around and saw no one with them any more, except Jesus only" (Mark 9:8). "And when the voice had spoken, Jesus was found alone" (Luke 9:36). The pillars of the old covenant economy, Moses and Elijah, leave the scene and Jesus only remains as the focus, underscoring the words from the cloud, "Hear Him!" Matthew Henry notes:

> Whoever would know the mind of God must hearken to Christ; for by Him God has spoken in these last days. This voice from heaven has made all the sayings of Christ as authentic as if they had been spoken out of the cloud.

God does here, as it were, turn us over to Christ for all the revelations of His mind.

The Concealment. After this remarkable and unforgettable experience, "He gave them orders not to relate to anyone what they had seen until the Son of Man should rise from the dead" (Mark 9:9). As the New Testament elsewhere notes (John 2:22), the resurrection of Christ was a crucial turning point for the disciples' understanding to be opened up to the implications of the Messiah's appearance in history.

Some Implications

We are in desperate need of being Christ-centered in our living and outlook. It seems to me that the New Exodus in Christ is the pivotal foundation for understanding our Christian life under the New Covenant. Just as God's redemptive act in the Red Sea exodus gave shape to Israel's old covenant life, so Jesus' death, burial, and resurrection are the acts of God that inform our life in Jesus.

It appears to me that in the history of theology little attention has been paid to the "hear Him" which came from the Shekinah glory, especially in the realm of Kingdom living. Over the years I have read thousands of pages from books on Christian ethics. They assert that salvation is found only in Christ, but then write as if Exodus 20 is the only place where righteous behavior can be discovered. It is as if Christ has really nothing to say about how we must live. But the truth is that the saving event also commands us how to walk in a fallen world (Titus 2:11-21).

God made Himself crystal clear in the solemn events on that mountain. The Old Testament figures disappeared and only Jesus was left for the disciples to behold. The voice from the cloud approbated the Son and commanded us only to hear the voice of the Shepherd. Are we going to listen to the central message and lesson of the transfiguration? Is the New Exodus indeed a pivotal turning point in the history of redemption, not only for our salvation, but also for our ethics? There is little hope that our appreciation for the "new commandment" will deepen until we first reckon that New Covenant ethics are rooted in the saving act of Christ's New Exodus.

THE NEW COMMANDMENT: "LOVE ONE ANOTHER, AS I HAVE LOVED YOU"

In John 13 Jesus shows by word and example that the behavior of His people is connected to and flows out of His decease, or *exodus*. As the old covenant was founded upon the saving action of God in the Red Sea exodus, so the New Covenant is ratified by the saving purpose of God in the exodus of Christ. The old covenant was sealed by the sprinkling of blood. The New Covenant is put into effect by the decease (exodus) of Christ through the shedding of His blood. The very act of self-sacrifice on Christ's part both redeemed His people and revealed to them how to please Him in their living. By examining John 13, we will see that our ethics must be rooted in Jesus Christ.

The Crucial Nature of John 13-17

As Jesus was on the eve of His exodus He shared those issues closest to His heart with the disciples and the Father. Of all things He could have uttered as His final words on earth, He chose what is recorded for us in John 13-17. We do well, therefore, to give heed to what might rightly be called the "heart of Christ" found in these discourses. John 13:1 introduces Jesus' words and actions in this manner:

> Now before the feast of the Passover, Jesus knowing His hour [exodus] had come that He should depart out of this world to the Father, having loved His own who were in the world, He loved them to the end.

The Action of Christ (John 13:3-9)

In this section the Lord of Glory humbles Himself to wash the feet of His disciples. His action is all the more striking when placed in the context of Jesus' reflection upon His Messianic mission: "knowing that the Father had given all things into His hands, and that He had come forth from God, and was going back to God." The One who could command the armies of heaven to do His bidding, and could rightly command humans to worship at His feet, instead assumes the position of a lowly servant, "pouring water into the basin and washing the disciples' feet."

Peter asked, "Lord, do you wash my feet?" Jesus responds. "What I do you do not realize now, but you shall understand in the future." This remark highlights the connection of His resurrection and His sending of the Holy Spirit to the opening up of their understanding to the implications of His incarnation (cf. John 2:22; 7:39; Luke 24:32, 44-45).

The Instruction of Christ (John 13:12-17)

The singular significance of this foot-washing event is underscored by the fact that Jesus not only performs a deed before their eyes, but then unequivocally interprets this action. "You call Me Teacher and Lord; and you are right; for so I am. If I then, the Lord and Teacher, washed your feet, you ought also to wash one another's feet. For I give you an example that you also should do as I did to you."

Of all the lessons Christ could have impressed upon His disciples He chose this model of servanthood. Above all else He wished for His people to be a kingdom of foot-washers. The greatest in Christ's realm would be the one who was the slave of all. Christ enforces the command to a life of servanthood by His own example. Jesus' earthly existence was the supreme paradigm of giving one's life for others. After the pouring out of the Spirit on the day of Pentecost, the apostles deepened appreciation, understanding and practice of this servant perspective is reflected in John's exclamation: "We know love by this, that He laid down His life for us [the indicative]; and we ought to lay down our lives for the brethren" [the imperative] (1 John 3:16).

Jesus makes it clear that blessedness comes by obedience to the imperative to serve others. "If you know these things, you are blessed if you do them." As John points out, love must be expressed concretely in sacrificial actions, or it is just empty talk (1 John 3:18). The way of blessedness is not to be like the Gentiles who crave after power and glory, but rather to meet the needs of others as Jesus did.

The Commandment of Christ (John 13:31-34)

In this section Jesus focuses on His impending death. In His departure, His exodus, both the Father and the Son will be glorified. "I am with you a little while longer. You shall seek Me, as I said to the Jews, 'where I am going you cannot come,' now I say to you." In the very near future Jesus is going to be physically removed from the disciples. In the setting of this announcement of the New Exodus, Jesus issues a New

Covenant mandate: "A new commandment I give to you, that you love one another as I have loved you, that you also love one another."

A question of pivotal significance is, What is "new" about this command to love since it is embedded in the Old Testament, for example, in Leviticus 19:18? It is "new" because it flows out of a New Exodus accomplished by the shed blood of the Lamb of God. The touchstone of love in the text is, "Even as I have loved you." Therein is the newness revealed. What is the reference point for love among the brethren? By what standard are we to love one another? What is the criterion for our love? "As I…."

The New Commandment arises out of the New Exodus. The New Exodus brings a command to love which is new, not in the sense that it just dropped out of heaven, but in connection to the advance of redemptive history to the solemn moment of Jesus' departure. Christ's giving of Himself for His friends is the specific foundation for the New Commandment (1 John 15:12-14).

After much reading in the field of Christian ethics, it is my opinion that theologians have rightly pointed to the finished work of Jesus Christ for salvation, but have wrongly sent New Covenant believers back to the demands upon Israel based on the old exodus, instead of starting with the New Commandment rooted on the New Exodus.

Walter Chantry typifies this pattern when he dogmatically asserts:

> Our Lord defined love by reference to the law. The repetition on this point is striking: "If you love Me, keep My commandments" (John 14:15); "He that has My commandments and keeps them, he it is that loves Me" (John

14:21). Love cannot be expressed without the guidelines of the law.[8]

Instead of seeing loving obedience as defined by the act of Christ in the New Exodus, it is assumed that only Exodus 20 can prescribe what is "right." When Jesus said "keep My commandments" it is assumed that He had in view precepts from Moses and not from Himself. But we learned in the transfiguration that the voice of the Father said "Listen to My Son," and they then saw "Jesus only." The truth is that Jesus means keep all My commandments that flow out of the singular New Commandment to love one another "as I have loved you" in the New Exodus.

The Observation of Christ (John 13:35)

On the basis of the New Commandment Christ marks the practice of it as of crucial importance: "By this all people will know that you are My disciples if you have love one to another." The effective witness of God's people hinges directly on their visible demonstration of love one to another. The Lord Jesus did not say, "By your creeds, doctrines, ornate church buildings, and elaborate programs people will know that you are My disciples." You can be a great preacher, give money to the poor or have your body burned for a cause, but if love for the brethren is not present, these things mean nothing. The true badge of gospel power is fervent love among brothers and sisters in Christ.

If we are candid, must we not admit that the church's witness has been tragically tarnished by our lack of love for one another? If this is the case, does this indicate that we have not been impacted as we should by the "As I have loved you" of the New Commandment?

The Pattern of Redemptive History

God has stretched out His arm of power on two occasions to create covenant peoples. The first was the exodus out of Egypt when the Lord parted the Red Sea and set Israel apart from the nations. The second was accomplished at Golgotha when Christ uttered, "It is finished." In a New Exodus He purchased the church of God with His own blood. After Israel came over dry land, the old covenant was sealed by Moses' sprinkling of blood. In the context of His baptism in suffering, Christ sealed the New Covenant with His blood.

In both the old and the New exodus the same pattern emerges. Only after the redemptive event are obligations for covenant living set forth. In both cases, the redemptive action of God in an exodus supplies the basis for the ethical response of God's people.

Old Covenant

- *Redemptive Event:* Red Sea Exodus, "I am the Lord your God who brought you out of the land of Egypt, out of the house of slavery" (Exodus 20:2).

- *Ethical Demand on Israel:* "You shall have no other Gods before Me," etc. (Exodus 20:2); "All that the Lord has spoken we will do!" (Exodus 19:8)

New Covenant

- *Redemptive Event:* Golgotha Exodus, "Even as I have loved you" (John 13:34; 15:12-13).

- *Ethical Demand on Body of Christ:* "Love one another" (John 13:34; 15:12-13); "If you love Me, you will keep My commandments (John 14:15)

THE NEW SPIRIT: "I WILL COME TO YOU"

The backdrop of Israel's apostasy from the Lord gave rise for the prophets to speak of "New" things to come with the advent of Christ. The apostasy of Israel set the stage for the prophetic utterances concerning a new age — a new *covenant,* a new *Spirit.* The old covenant was broken, and God promises that a new covenant will be established (Jer. 31:31-34) Stony hearts will be replaced with pliable, fleshly hearts (Ezek. 36:26). In Messiah's age there will be a new Spirit (Ezek. 36:27). John Bright in 1953 captured the ethos of the "new" the prophets foretold:

Indeed, it was during [Israel's] Exile that [the hope of God's kingdom] was given its profoundest expression…The prophets, especially Jeremiah and Ezekiel, had prepared for the day when, the external forms of religion having been swept away, faith would have to go on without them…[They] looked for] the birth of a new nation with the Spirit of God in its heart…[where] there flows a stream of living water…A "new thing" is about to come to pass, so stupendous that it will overshadow even the great things of the past…But what is this "new thing"?…It is the imagery of the Exodus. Israel is to experience a new Exodus. To speak of a new Exodus could therefore mean only a new beginning, and a New Covenant, which Jeremiah spoke of…[The suffering Servant] is the central actor in the "new thing" that is about to take place; he is, we might say, the "new Moses" in the new Exodus now shortly to begin (*The Kingdom of God: The Biblical Concept and Its Meaning For the Church*, Abingdon, 1953, pp. 127-155).

It was this tension in Israel's life that gave rise to hope for the times of refreshing from the Messiah (Acts 3.18-26).

In the midst of a rebellious nation, the promise is given by Joel, and God, "I will pour out My Spirit on all peoples," "I will pour out my Spirit in those days" (Joel 2:28-29). But this promise could not be fulfilled until Isaiah 53 was first completed. The Messiah had to suffer and be glorified in the resurrection *before* the Spirit could come (John 7:39).

After being consecrated to His Messianic, priestly work by John's baptism, the Spirit comes down upon Jesus (Matt. 3:16), and the Father's approval is sealed in the words, "This is my beloved Son, in whom I am well pleased" (Matt. 3:17).

But also at the outset, what does John the Baptist announce will be one of the central goals of the Messiah's work? *The obtaining of the Spirit for the New Israel will be His crowning achievement* (Matt. 3:11; Luke 3:16; cf., Richard Gaffin, Jr., *Perspectives on Pentecost,* Baker, 1979, pp. 14-16). But, before the living waters can flow from the innermost being of believers, Jesus had to be baptized with suffering Himself (Mark 10:38; Luke 12:50). When John comments that "the Holy Spirit was not [yet]," obviously he does not mean that there was no activity of the Spirit until the Day of Pentecost (John 7:39), But we can say that the "absoluteness" of this remark, "not yet," indicates the magnitude of the future coming of the Spirit — it is as though, from a redemptive-historical standpoint, there was no Holy Spirit until after the resurrection.

Further, it is clear that in John's mind this future manifestation of the Spirit was dependent on the completion of the death, burial, and resurrection of our Lord. Only after Jesus was accepted from the dead, and declared to be the Son of God with power (Rom. 1:4), could the Spirit be sent to His waiting people. Thus, in Peter's message on the Day of

Pentecost he interprets the appearance of the Spirit in power as "what was spoken of through the prophet Joel" (Acts 2:16). But Peter specifically designates the Pentecostal phenomena as an *act of Christ:* "therefore having been exalted to the right hand of God, and having received from the Father the promise of the Spirit, He has poured forth this which you both see and hear" (Acts 2:33).

The New Israel is not the recipient of covenantal tablets of stone, but of an inward inscription: "and I will put my Spirit within you and cause you to walk in my statutes, and you will be careful to observe my ordinances" (Ezek. 36:27). The law could not bring a reign of righteousness (Rom. 8:3), but the new covenant does (Jer. 31:33-34; 2 Cor. 3:9) The old covenant was administered outwardly on tablets of stone (2 Cor. 3:3,7). The new covenant is administered inwardly on human hearts (2 Cor. 3:3). Physical Israel possessed a law (canon) that was a ministry of condemnation (2 Cor. 3:9); spiritual Israel possesses a rule (canon) of the Spirit that brings a righteous liberty (Gal. 6:15-16; 5:1,13, 2 Cor. 3:17). An administration of law came by Moses; an administration of grace and truth has broken into history in the Incarnation (John 1:14-18). Old Israel broke their covenant (Jer. 31:32); New Israel keeps the "new" commandment of the new covenant — they love Him in obedience because He first loved them (John 13:34; 14:15; 1 John 4:19).

John 16:8-11

The N.T. teaches that in salvation the Spirit reveals Christ to the sinner's heart. In John 16:8-11, Jesus teaches that after Pentecost He will send the Spirit to convince people of the sin of unbelief, of the righteousness of Christ, and the judgment of Satan. These three elements—sin, righteousness and judgment — are all approached in a Christ-centered way.

But in John 16:8-11 there is *nothing* said about the Spirit taking the law to "slay" sinners, and then revealing Christ to them. Rather, the Spirit is said to take the things of Christ and disclose them to people (John 16:13-15). Indeed, the other Scriptures in the N.T. referring to the purpose and function of the law nowhere teach that it is designed to be the means of spiritually convicting persons in preparation for the gospel.

"The work of the Spirit in revealing Christ," which focuses on John 16:8-11, was called by Spurgeon, "a compendium of the work of the Spirit of God." George Smeaton calls this passage "the most conclusive passage on the Spirit's work in connection with conversion in the whole compass of Scripture. This passage contains a full and exhaustive description of the Spirit's work in the application of redemption" *(The* Doctrine of the *Holy Spirit* [1882], Banner of Truth, 1961, pp. 172, 173).

We must note, first of all, that the promised convicting work of the Spirit is based upon the saving action of *God* in Christ (John 16:5, 7). The Father sent the Son. After the Son had suffered and had been glorified in the resurrection, He sent the Spirit to a waiting church (Acts 2:33). The work of the Spirit, therefore, is a *result of* and *related to* the saving work of Christ. The Spirit's work centers on Christ. "The *subject* on which the gift of the Spirit is now designed and fitted to shed a clear and convincing light is the character and offices of Christ" (James Buchanan, *The Office and Work of the Holy Spirit* [1843], Banner of Truth, 1966, p. 27).

The Holy Spirit's work is not Spirit-centered and does

not call attention to itself. The Spirit testifies of *Christ* (John 16:14-15). This truth calls into serious question much of the contemporary teaching and practice in the charismatic movement. Too often there is such a focus on the *Spirit, His* gifts, *His* manifestations, and *His* presence that Christ is placed on the sidelines. This grieves the Spirit, for He points people to Christ, not to Himself.

Christ says that after Pentecost the Spirit will convince humans of "sin, righteousness and judgment." This will occur in connection with *gospel* proclamation. "These three lessons or doctrines have reference to one and the same great subject, namely, Christ" (Buchanan, p. 28).

"Of Sin"

It is not sin in *general* that is here isolated, but specifically the sin of *not believing* in *Christ*. "Sin" in this verse equals — according to "the true interpreter of His own words" — not believing in the Son (Smeaton, p.176). In 1 John 3:23, all that God requires is boiled down to, "this is His command-ment, that we believe in the name of His Son."

Unbelief is the specific sin that the Spirit will bring peo-ple to see in conversion. Why is unbelief given as if it were the "only sin"? Because while a person continues in unbelief all of his other sins are retained; but when people believe in Christ all of their other sins are remitted (Smeaton, p. 178). A person may feel guilty about many sins (drunkenness, adultery, stealing, etc.), but such conviction avails nothing until the Spirit convinces him of the fatal sin of unbelief.

The specific ministry of the Spirit in this text is to bring peo-ple to an awareness of their unbelief in Christ.

When carnal men…talk of sin, I suppose they generally

mean shameful crimes or gross violations of the Divine law; but when the Holy Spirit comes to convict of sin, he reveals to people another sin, of which naturally they think nothing — viz., that of *not believing in Jesus* (Charles Ross, *The Inner Sanctuary— An Exposition of John 13 - 17* [1888], Banner of Truth, 1967, pp. 159-l60).

Thus, in this passage — "the *locus classicus* . . . as to the way in which the Spirit applies redemption" (Smeaton, pp.175-176) — the Spirit is said to convict men and women with reference to the things of Christ. As Leon Morris cogently observed:

> It should not be overlooked that all three aspects of the work of the Holy Spirit dealt with in these verses are looked at in a Christ-centered way. Sin, righteousness and judgment are all to be understood in a way that relates to the Christ *(Commentary on John,* p. 699).

Is it not significant that, if a "law-work" is so important and necessary, this passage nowhere states or implies that the Spirit will use the law to drive people to Christ?

Rom. 8:23—"and not only this, but also we ourselves, having the first- fruits of the Spirit, even we ourselves groan within ourselves, waiting eagerly for our adoption as *sons, the redemption of our body."*

This text presents the *future* dimensions of the Spirit's work in believers. We live in a *tension:* we are in-between the already and the not yet. The "first-fruits," the "earnest" (Eph. 1:14) are ours, but what awaits us is really our hope (Gal. 5:5). The Spirit's work in us now is the intrusion of the age to come into this age (cf. Geerhardus Vos, "The Eschatological Aspect of the Pauline Conception of the Spirit," *Redemptive History and Biblical Interpretation,* pp. 91-125). We possess the "down payment," but await the full harvest when we shall see Him as He is (1 John 3:2). The sufferings of this age, therefore, are not worthy to be compared with the glory of seeing Jesus face-to-face (Rom 8:18).

It is this basic consideration of where we are in redemptive history that determines our outlook on life and its struggles. As Richard Longnecker put it, *the Christian life is "expressed in a situation of temporal tension between what is already a fact and what has yet to be realized"* (*The Ministry and Message of St. Paul,* Zondervan, p. 101).

The Spirit's work in the body is Christ-centered. The Lord Jesus specifically said that after His physical departure, the Holy Spirit would come to the church and "glorify Me" (John 16:14). The Spirit *never* points to Himself; He *always* directs persons to Christ as revealed in the Word. The contemporary charismatic movement has too often so emphasized the Spirit, spiritual gifts, and spiritual manifestations, that it has perpetrated a false Spirit-centered "gospel." But the Spirit testifies of *Christ,* not to Himself.

When the local church assembles, Christ must be central — not gifts, not preachers, not pulpits, not priesthood, not "sacraments." The thing to be most coveted is *the presence of Christ in the person of the Spirit* (Matt. 18:20; John 14:18). The Word and Spirit come together to glorify the Son — and it is only in this light that the place of the priesthood, the ministry of the Word, the Lord's Supper/Baptism, and gifts can be properly understood.

It is obvious that God has designed our corporate gatherings so that the vertical (God/people) and horizontal (people/people) dimensions come together. Spirit-led meetings will direct the saints to lift up Christ in all directions. Our gathering together to express the Lord is not in conflict with our exhorting of one another (Heb. 10:25; Col. 3:16). But most traditions so emphasize the vertical perspective that the horizontal is virtually unknown. Some traditions are so horizontally focused that the vertical is actually peripheral. But in true gatherings the Holy Spirit brings the two great commandments together — love to God and love to brothers and sisters. Together, we speak to both God and one another. We can judge the work of the Spirit in our midst by the proper balance of these two mandatory dimensions. My guess is that most churches need more of the *horizontal* expression in their gatherings.

The Spirit's work in the body is charismatic. By "charismatic" I mean that the resurrected Christ has "led captivity captive and given gifts to His people" (Eph. 4:8). The gifts are not ends in themselves, but are given to each member for the common benefit of the body (1 Cor. 12:7). I am suggesting that various notions have contributed to a playing down of the proper charismatic nature of the church. For example, we have so focused on one ministry — "the pastor" — that we have not been able to focus rightly on the body (1 Cor. 12:14). Granted, not all gifts are of a public nature; but we have wrongly functioned as though only *one* gift is public. In an open gathering of the saints, all are able to function publicly as the Spirit leads (1 Cor. 14:26).

"Ordained Ministry"/"Multiple Ministry"

J. I. Packer noted:

> Puritan attention when discussing gifts was dominated by their interest in the ordained ministry, and hence in those particular gifts which qualify a one for ministerial

office, and questions about other gifts to other persons were rarely raised ("Puritans," p. 15).

In light of the principle of multiple participation we find in the N.T. church gatherings, on what basis can Packer assert that "in its regular life, the official ministry is central" in the local church (Packer, "Puritans," p. 21). As far as I can tell, the main effect of the "official ministry" has been to stifle the plurality of gifts and contributions of the many members. Packer suggests that the Puritans were concerned "for authenticity and reality in the life of the Church and Christians" ("Puritans," p. 24). However, I cannot conceive of such authenticity and reality coming to valid expression through the power of the Spirit, when the basic *charismatic* nature of the church is side-stepped.

The Spirit's work in the body is congregationally oriented. Much could be said here, but I would like to focus on the reality that *the Spirit-inspired New Covenant letters were addressed to ekklesias (assemblies), not to leaders.* Even the epistle sent to an individual (Philemon) mentions "the ekklesia that meets in your home." As the Spirit works to resolve problems, the final step is "take it to the ekklesia" (Matt. 18:15-18). Nothing is mentioned about "leaders" taking charge of matters. Paul saw the Spirit moving in *ekklesias* as the setting for the life of Christ to come to expression in multifaceted ways (1 Cor. 5-6).

New Exodus/New Commandment/New Spirit

The content of systematic theologies in the past several hundred years reveals that the three themes mentioned above have been given almost zero attention. The "newness" of the New Covenant has been muted. It was like little changed after Jesus appeared in history. Theological enterprise from AD 200 to AD 1900 was essentially old covenant-based. There has been little sensitivity, until around 1950, to the reality that history has moved from an *obsolete old covenant* to the *living waters of the New Covenant*, and that with Jesus came a *new creation*, a *new exodus*, a *new commandment*, and a *new Spirit*.

As I have meditated on various Biblical patterns and teachings in light of the history of theology, one central thought repeatedly comes to mind: in most theological expression and argumentation, there has been a "flat Bible" proof-texting methodology which has not done justice to the progress of redemptive history. A statement by Herman Ridderbos has kept ringing in my mind: "the new creation brings a new canon, a new standard of judgment along with it. *This is above all redemptive-historical in character"* (*Paul: An Outline of His Theology,* Eerdmans, 1975, p. 286). Richard Gaffin, Jr., makes the following pointed and significant observations:

It is difficult to deny that in the orthodox tradition justice has not been done to the historical character of the Bible, either in terms of its origin or its contents. There has been and continues to be a tendency to view Scripture as a quarry of proof-texts for the building of a dogmatic edifice, as a collection of moral principles for the construction of a system of ethics…Inscripturated revelation never stands by itself. It is always concerned either explicitly or implicitly with redemptive accomplishment…In other words, the specific unity of Scripture is redemptive-historical in nature…It does not appear to me, however, that the *methodological* significance of this correlation has been reflected upon sufficiently ("Contemporary Hermeneutics in the Study of the New

Testament," *Studying the NT Today,* Ed. John H. Skilton, Presbyterian & Reformed, Vol.1, pp. 15-16).

> God, after He spoke long ago to the fathers in the prophets in many portions and in many ways, in these last days has spoken to us in His Son, whom He appointed heir of all things, through whom also He made the world. And He is the radiance of His glory and the exact representation of His nature, and upholds all things by the word of His power. When He had made purification of sins, He sat down at the right hand of the Majesty on high (Hebrews 1:1-3). ∎

Endnotes:

1. Werner Elert, *Law and Gospel,* Fortress Press, 1987, pp. 8, 47.

2. Cf. W.B Selbie, "The Influence of the Old Testament on Puritanism" *BRR,* Autumn 1979, pp. 13-21 ($1.75); Conrad Cherry, ed., *God's New Israel: Religious Interpretations of American Destiny,* Prentice-Hall, 1971, 375pp.

3. Cf. Harald Sahlin, "Christ Our 'Exodus': The Fulfillment of An Old Testament Theme," *ST,* Summer 1985, pp. 3-6, 34; Hamish Swanston, "The Exodus In The New Testament," *The Community Witness: An Exploration of Some of the Influences at Work in the N.T. Community & Its Writings,* Sheed & Ward, 1967, pp. 49-53.

4. *The Gospel According to Mark* [1858]. Banner of Truth, 1960, p. 234.

5. *The Life and Times of Jesus the Messiah* [1886], Eerdmans, 1962. Vol.2, p. 93.

6. G.F. McClear, *A Classbook of N.T. History,* p. 222.

7. David Smith, *The Days of His Flesh,* p. 274.

8. *Today's Gospel: Authentic or Synthetic?,* Banner of Truth, pp. 40-41. In this context it is clear that by "Law" Chantry means the Ten Commandments in Exodus 20 (cf. footnote, p. 35).

"LOVE ONE ANOTHER—AS I HAVE LOVED YOU"

JON ZENS

This piece was written in connection with the 1980 Council on Baptist Theology, held in Plano, Texas. It was published in the Summer, 1980, Baptist Reformation Review, *just in time for me to bring it to the conference.*

In this article I wish to submit that *the Lord Jesus Christ* stands as the focus of our obedience. Christ in us—the One who spoke words of life and finished a redemptive work—brings us to lovingly follow Him (cf. Willis P. De Boer, *The Imitation of Paul* [J.H. Kok: Kampen, 1962], pp. 55-57: "the imitation [of Christ] was rooted in the fellowship and union with Christ and sprang forth from it…The 'ought' arises from what their Lord has done for them").

Because of its foundational character, our beginning point will be John 13:34-35. In this passage we are confronted with *one* commandment. All other commandments are related to this "new" demand, a demand which is intimately rooted to His "obedience unto death" (Phil.2:8).

JOHN 13:34—"LOVE ONE ANOTHER AS I HAVE LOVED YOU"

There is a certain "specialness" attached to these final discourses of our Lord in John 13-17. They are His last words on earth. It is apparent that just before His "hour" came (13:1). Jesus is confronting His inner circle with matters of critical importance. Therefore, it is incumbent upon us to pay close attention to Jesus' words.

The Lord Jesus was Lord of all (13:3). At this point in time, He could have rightly commanded *worship* of His person from these disciples. But, no, the King of Kings "took a towel and girded himself…and began to wash the disciples' feet" (13:4-5). Wonder of wonders, the King takes the position of a *lowly servant*! Does not this action highlight the lesson our Lord is communicating here? He wants them *more than anything else* to see that loving servant-hood is foundational in His kingdom. Our Lord does not act here as an aloof King who is ministered unto, but does not minister; rather, He calls His disciples to do *what He has just performed before their eyes* (13:14-16). This action of Christ stands as a constant "example" which is to serve as a model for Christian behaviour until the end of the age.

Would we be "happy," or blessed? Then we must be captured by this "singular" action of Christ and live in light of its demand among our brothers and sisters (13:17). The *only* way to Christian blessedness is to be a *servant* (Matt. 20:26).

"AS I HAVE LOVED YOU"

However, the "example" of Christ is not done in a vacuum. This humbling of the Son is symbolic of the imminent baptism of suffering to occur at Golgotha (De Boer, p. 55). This is brought out in John 15:12-13. After repeating the "new commandment," Christ connects the "as I have loved you" with the laying down of His life for His friends.

This supreme act of love on the cross clearly becomes the reference point, the starting point, and the touchstone of all Christian obedience. Our love to one another is not just a reaction to the general love of God; rather it is specifically a love which is related to the act of God in giving Christ for us (1 John 4:9-11). The multifaceted commandments which inform believers of their responsibilities (John14:15) *are to be approached through singular commandment to "love one another, as I have loved you."*

ARE WE CONSTRAINED BY THIS LOVE?

Brethren, I suggest that if we miss this point we miss everything. If we come to any duty and commandment, apart from the love of God shed abroad in our hearts by the Spirit (Rom. 5:5), we have either landed on, or are dangerously close to the shores of legalism. Jesus reveals that the most important perspective to grasp is that the pervasive demand on the life which the gospel brings must be carried out in love—a love that has arisen in the heart in reaction to God's love for us in Christ. It is this kind of love alone which provides the impetus for Christian action. How conscious are you in your daily living of this "as I have loved you" perspective? Are you convinced that this display of love on the cross is "sufficient incentive" to restrain you from sin and to move you toward holy living (Dennis Winter, "Motivation in Christian Behavior," (*Law, Morality and the Bible* [IVP, 1978], eds. Bruce Kaye and Gordon Wenham, p. 212)?

"BY THIS SHALL ALL PEOPLE KNOW THAT YOU ARE MY DISCIPLES"

The importance of this love perspective is further seen by Christ's words in 13:35. The characteristic which He isolates as being the most necessary in terms of the world *visibly observing* the reality of Christ is love among the brothers and sisters. Not our sound doctrine, not our creeds, not our persuasive preaching, not our impressive buildings, not our elaborate denominational programs, not our huge numbers—*but concrete love among believers.* Historically in the Reformed tradition the three "marks" of a "true church" are:

1. the Word preached;

2. the ordinances properly administered;

3. discipline practiced.

But a church could have all those "marks" and miss *the* "mark" that Christ says is the only one that really counts. Without love, all is vain (1 Cor. 13:1-3). We need the love our Lord described in 13:34 more than anything else.

A NEW COVENANT.

This love of God manifested in Christ's crucifixion constituted the sealing of a covenant, the new covenant (1.Cor. 11:25). The old covenant had been "broken" (Jer. 31:32). The new covenant is put into effect legally on "better promises" (Heb. 8:6; cf. my "Believer's Rule of Life," *BRR*, Vol.8. #4, 1979, p. 18).

A NEW COMMANDMENT

It is in connection with the blood of the new covenant that Jesus issues the "new commandment." It is imperative for us to see that with a covenant comes a demand upon the covenant people. The old covenant was consecrated with blood (Heb. 9:18), and with it came the requirements upon Israel. Can we not also see also that the new covenant, sealed with the blood of God's spotless Lamb, brought with it the "new commandment" to love one another?

It is impossible to grasp what is "new" about the new commandment unless the *historical element* in John 13:34 is considered. The command to love is *old* (Lev. 19:18). But the command for brethren to *love as Christ loved them at the cross is new*. In other words, in the text it is a *strictly historical factor* that renders the command to love *new*. The old covenant brought with it a law (Exod. 20); the new covenant brought with it a "new commandment" (13:34; 15:12). This command flows out of the death of Christ: "love…as I have loved you."

Thus, as Rudolph Stier pointed out, "to a covenant belongs a law-giving" (*The Words of the Lord Jesus*, 1872, Vol. 6, p. 161). The "law of Christ" is the law of love (Gal. 6:2). The Christian is to order his life in the light of the all-encompassing demand of love (1Cor. 13:4-7).

A NEW EXODUS

To graphically see the relationship of covenant and law, we can compare the redemptive events which separated Israel and the church to God. The mighty exodus out of Egypt is singled out as that which is *prior* to the demands on Israel (Exodus 20:2). The gracious act of God *comes before* the covenant commandments. But the Egyptian exodus was *typical* of an exodus which would be accomplished in the Messianic age. F.F. Bruce observes:

Jesus' contemporaries freely identified Him as a second Moses—the expectation of a second Moses played an important part in popular eschatology at the time—and with the expectation of a second Moses went very naturally the expectation of a second exodus (*The N.T. Development of O.T. Themes,* p. 49; cf. Robert D. Brinsmead. *Verdict.* Feb., 1979, p. 32; Nov. 1979, pp. 18, 21).

Thus it should not surprise us that with the mighty deliverance effected by Christ in His death, burial and resurrection, came a pervasive call to loving servanthood (John 13:14-17; 15:12-13). Arising out of the loving act of Christ is the summons to love (cf. Robin Nixon, "The Universality of the Concept of Law," *Law, Morality,* p. 114).

JOHN 13:7B—"WHAT I DO YOU DO NOT UNDERSTAND NOW, BUT YOU SHALL KNOW IN THE FUTURE"

It was not until *after* the resurrection of Christ, and specifically after the giving of the promised Spirit on the Day of Pentecost, that the apostles came to more deeply and concretely understand the implications of Christ's washing of their feet (cf. John 2:22). John in his First Epistle exhorts his readers in terms which echo the John 13 example of Christ. "Hereby we perceive the love of God, because He laid down His life for us [redemptive event]: and we ought to lay down our lives for the brethren [moral demand]" (1 John 3:16). "In this was manifested the love of God toward us, because God sent His only begotten Son into the world…to be the propitiation for our sins [redemptive event]. Beloved, if God so loved us [at the cross], we ought to love one another [moral demand]" (1 John 4:9-11).

Is it not clear enough that when the N.T. writers wish to press duties upon Christians, their starting point is the *cross*—"as I have loved you"? This is not the *sole* approach to unfold life in the N.T., but it is certainly the most basic, foundational and important approach. We can say such a thing because Jesus taught this perspective at the end of His earthly ministry. Bruce Kaye summarizes all of this by saying:

> The fundamental idea of the Christian as someone in relationship with Christ provides not only the best way to see the basis of the Christian's ethical life, but also the form and content of that life ("Law and Morality in the Epistles of the N.T.," *Law, Morality*, p. 84; cf. p. 85).

Perhaps in the light of John 13:34-35 we can understand why so much material in the Gospels focuses on the final "hour" of Christ. John Blanchard points out that two-fifths of Matthew, three-fifths of Mark, one third of Luke, and about one half of John "record the events surrounding the week Jesus was crucified" (*Right With God* [Moody, 1978], p. 80; cf. De Boer, p. 67).

Having laid this foundation, let us turn briefly to the Old Testament, and more extensively to the New Testament, and see if this Christ-centered perspective is not all the more confirmed.

DEUT. 18:15-19—"TO HIM YOU SHALL HEARKEN"

The awesomeness and fearfulness of the appearance of God on Sinai here provides the rationale for a mediating Prophet through whom God will decisively speak (cf. Heb.12:18-21). This future prophet is to be (1) from Israel; (2) like Moses in some sense; and (3) heard with reverence because he speaks words from God.

Jesus, of course, is this promised Prophet. God spoke in a final way through Him in these last days (Heb. 1:2). At the Messiah's baptism and transfiguration, God the Father verbally expressed His approval of this unique person: "This is my beloved Son, in whom I am well pleased; hear Him" (Matt. 3:17; 17:5). Obviously, these heavenly words echo the promise of Deut. 18:15, 18. After the resurrection, Peter sees the fulfilment of the Deut. 18 Prophet in the Christ: "Him you shall hear in all things whatever he shall say to you" (Acts 3:32; cf. my "'This Is My Beloved Son…Hear Him,'" *BRR*, 1978, 7:4, pp. 15-52).

Thus, as the cross becomes the reference point for our love, so the historic person of Christ as Prophet becomes the reference point for our ears. We are to listen to the Son, for He has the words from God (cf. John 6:68-69). Even Moses points away from himself, and commands us to hear the prophet who is "like unto him." This, of course, does not mean that we stop our ears to Moses because we are told to hear the Son, for if we listen rightfully to Moses he testifies of Christ (John 5:39, 46; Luke 24:27, 44). With the coming of the Prophet of whom Moses wrote, we approach Moses *through Him* who has all authority in heaven and earth. Moses will be our accuser if we read the O.T. apart from Christ (John 5:45; 2 Cor. 3:15-16).

'Tis the long expected Prophet
David's Son, yet David's Lord;
By His Son God now has spoken:
'Tis the true and faithful Word (*Trinity Hymnal,* #192)

LAW THROUGH MOSES, JOHN 1:17A

As "promise" is characteristic of the Abrahamic covenant, "law" is characteristic of the Sinaitic covenant. This law was inflexible, and demanded "curse" on everything in it at all times (Gal. 3:10). This administration of law was added 430 years after the Abrahamic covenant (Gal. 3:17). It was added "because of transgressions" (Gal. 3:19), and so that the "offence might abound" (Rom. 5:20), until the seed [Christ] should come" (Gal. 3:19). This administration of law, therefore, "is not something that is of fundamental importance to us. It is something additional, it is something that has come in for the time being, for a particular function" (D. Martyn Lloyd-Jones, *Romans: An Exposition of Chapter 5* [London: Banner of Truth, 1971], p. 285). The book of Hebrews makes it clear that the law could make nothing perfect, and that something "better" was necessary to effect redemption and forgiveness. From the new covenant perspective, it is retrogressive and dangerous to go back under the "beggarly elements," and "yoke of bondage" of the Mosaic covenant (Gal. 4:9; 5:1). This Mosaic administration was, like the Egyptian bondage, a stiff taskmaster that offered no relief. Thus, while the law (*as Scripture*) is "good," it is (*as covenant*) connected to the reign and strength of sin (Rom. 6:14; 1 Cor. 15:56).

As to its proper purpose, it is "not made for a righteous person," but for the ungodly (1 Tim. 1:8-9). If people were left with "do this and live" there would be no hope, but in the fullness of time, there came…

GRACE AND TRUTH BY JESUS CHRIST. JOHN 1:17B

There is something effected in the historical manifestation of Christ which was unattainable under Moses' administration of law. This "something" is described in v. 16 as "grace upon grace" (Greek, *charin anti charitos*). Most commentators see this phrase as similar to "faith to faith" (Rom. 1:17) and "glory to glory" (2 Cor. 3:18). The revelation of Christ brought an administration of "grace and truth." Why? Because He was the promised "seed" of Abraham, and the "prophet" promised by Moses. And, while the law is "not of faith" ("but do this and live"), the gospel is by faith, that it might be by grace (Rom. 4:16; Gal. 3:8,11).

The believer's life, then, is not initiated and sustained *by law*. Rather, it is in union with Christ, partaking by faith of His fullness, that we live a life "under grace," "grace upon grace." It is this "grace of God" which has historically appeared in Christ that teaches, or disciplines, us to "deny ungodliness and worldly lusts, that we should live soberly, righteously, and godly in this present age" (Titus 2:11-12). Again, we see that incentive for holy living arises out of our union with Him "who gave Himself for us," and is coming again to judge the living and the dead (Titus 2:13-14).

"THE FULLNESS OF TIME"

Bringing the three historical considerations we have isolated together, we can see the importance attached to *the historical appearance of Christ.* His coming in the fullness of time is the decisive event of redemptive history. The *crucifixion* both accomplished redemption and became the crucial reference point for Christian obedience. We must bring this Christ-centered perspective to our reflection upon the relationship of law and gospel.

Using Paul as an example, we find that he "evaluates the law completely from the vantage point of the new stage of the history of redemption in Christ" (A.J. Bandstra, *The Law and the Elements of the World,* p. 77). "Paul's doctrine of the law," therefore, "is developed from a purely Christological point of view" (G.B. Stevens, *The Pauline Theology* [New York, 1892], p. 171). W. Gutbrod crystallizes this point by saying:

> It is the cross of Jesus which determines for Paul his understanding of the outcome of the law. The whole of Paul's thought revolves around the proposition that the crucified Jesus is the Christ. In the same way it determines his attitude towards the law. *This alone* provides an intelligible, inherently necessary, connection between his affirmation and negation of the law (*Law,* [Adam & Charles Black, 1962], p. 106, emphasis mine; cf. also p. 119).

Thus, as Oscar Cullman observed, "without taking salvation history into account, we would have to regard Paul's teaching on the law as completely self-contradictory" (*Salvation in History,* [SCM Press, 1967], p. 335. It is interesting to note that Cullman says: "to my knowledge a comprehensive 'salvation-historical ethics' is still to be written" [p. 329]).

In order to highlight the pre-eminence of Christ, we will examine how several theological traditions have clouded our vision of the Son of God.

THE PURITAN TRADITION:

Thomas Watson. *The Ten Commandments* (1692; London, 1965)

The most obvious thing about Watson's approach to Christian duty is that he assumes that ethical fullness is to be found only in the Ten Commandments. Rather than starting with the redemptive event of the new covenant (the cross), he begins with the old exodus from Egypt. Instead of beginning with "as I have loved you," he begins with "I have brought you out of Egypt." To be sure, the Red Sea exodus *pointed* to a future exodus, but Watson makes it *and end in itself.* This illustrates the basic old covenant orientation of Puritanism.

Watson asserts that obedience to the Ten Commandments is the Christian's rule of life (p. 6.). He believes that "obedience [to it] must be in and through Christ" (p. 3). However, is this the approach of the N.T.? In terms of *starting point*, does the N.T. point the believer to life flowing out of the new exodus, or just refer him back to the Egyptian exodus mentioned in Exod. 20? In light of the advance of redemptive history, is it not mandatory to *begin* with the "new commandment" which is connected to the new covenant blood (of Christ)?

"DO THIS AND LIVE"

Another problem which surfaces is that since the Puritans viewed law strictly in terms of the Decalogue, there was a tendency to structure the gospel in terms of "do this and live." Obviously, their desire was to maintain the freeness of grace apart from works, but the formula that often came across was "*if* obedience, *then* blessing," which is the legal principle of the Mosaic covenant. For example, Watson says, "what are the great arguments or incentives to obedience? (1) Obedience makes us precious to God, his favorites…Would we have a blessing in our estates?…To obey is the best way to thrive in our estates [Deut. 28:1, 3, 5]" (pp. 4-5). Does the N.T. teach that we become precious to God by our obedience, or that we are precious to Him because we are *already* "accepted in the Beloved"?

In his section on "Love" (pp. 6-12), Watson sees the sum of the Decalogue as "love to God and neighbor," but he never discusses the "new commandment" to love one another, and only on two brief occasions mentions love as related to Christ's work (pp. 9, 11). Does this reflect sensitivity to the N.T. emphasis as found in 1 John 3:16, 4:9-11?

When dealing with the preface to the Ten Commandments (Exod. 20:1-2), Watson says that "all these words" refers to the "moral law," which is "the rule of life and manners" (p. 12). "Though the moral law be not a Christ to justify us," he says, "it is a rule to instruct us" (p. 12). To me, this implies that we need Christ to *justify us*, but we do not need Christ to *instruct* us, for all the instruction we need is in the Decalogue. But, as we have seen, the N.T. makes it clear that the person of Christ, especially the cross of Christ, is the *starting point of instruction in all areas of life.*

THE LAW AS "HEDGE"

Further, Watson sees the law of God "as a hedge to keep us within the bounds of sobriety and piety" (p. 13). But is it the case that those who are "sons" need the law as a "hedge"? Was the law not designed as a "hedge" for Israel *until the coming of Christ* (Gal. 3:25; 4:2)? This whole approach to law in the believer's life does not do justice to the status of believers as "new creations" who are not debtors to live after the flesh because they are "under grace" (Gal. 6:15; Rom. 8:12; 6:14).

Paul did not approach believers as if they were little children who needed all kinds of "hedges." Rather, he had *confidence* that God was at work in believers (Phil. 1:6). Paul fears for the Galatians because they observe days, and have come under beggarly elements (4:10-11). But, in the midst of all their serious problems, Paul expresses *hope*: "I have confidence in you through the Lord, that you will adopt no other view" (5:10). In 2 Thess. 3:4, Paul says "we have confidence in the Lord touching you, that you both do and will do the things which we command you." Likewise, Paul can write to Philemon: "Having confidence in your obedience I wrote to you, knowing that you will also do more than I say" (v. 21).

The way the N.T. approaches new life is through the "law of Christ," which is love. Believers are exhorted as responsible people who are expected to do the right things because they are sheep tuned into Christ's voice. And in those exhortations, the *dying of Christ* is the "sufficient incentive" (Winter, *Law, Morality*, pp. 211-212).

This "hedge" approach implies that if you leave believers alone there is no telling what they will do. But Paul's approach is otherwise. In Paul's letters the presumption is that believers will grow and develop in faith and character. They should become more able to make correct moral decisions, they must learn to discern what is important and what is not, and they are expected to develop in character as Christians (Kaye, *Law, Morality*, p. 89).

CAN THE LAW "SANCTIFY"?

"We say not," says Watson, "that he [the believer] is under the curse of the law, but [under] the commands. We say not the moral law is a Christ, but it is a star to lead to Christ. We say not that it saves, but sanctifies" (p. 13). To teach that the law is capable of sanctifying a believer is a dangerous notion, but nevertheless consistent with such emphasis on the centrality of law. Just how does a believer escape the curse of the law in justification yet remain under its full dominion in pursuing life in Christ?

NOT UNDER LAW, BUT UNDER LAW

This tension of the Christian being unable to fully obey the law, yet being required to obey it fully as a rule of life, is explained by Watson in the following specious way:

> In a true gospel-sense, we may so obey the moral law as to find acceptance. This gospel obedience consists in a real endeavor to observe the whole moral law. "I have done thy commandments" (Ps. 119:166); not, I have done all I should do, but I have done all I am able to do; and wherein my obedience comes short, I look up to the perfect righteousness and obedience of Christ, and hope for a pardon through his blood. This is to obey the moral law evangelically; which, though it be not to satisfaction, yet it is to acceptation…though we cannot, by our own strength, fulfil all these commandments, yet doing *quoad posse*, what we are able, the Lord has provided encouragement for us…Though we cannot exactly fulfil the moral law, yet God for Christ's sake will mitigate the rigor of the law, and accept of something less than he requires. God in the law requires exact obedience, yet will accept of sincere obedience; he will abate something of the degree, if there

be truth in the inward parts. He will see the faith, and pass by the failing. The gospel remits the severity of the moral law (pp. 16, 47).

The idea that the gospel waters down the rigor of the law is horrendous teaching. The N.T. never suggests that the rigors of the law can be mitigated under any circumstances. It appears that Watson is driven to reduce the demand of the law under the gospel in order to maintain it as a rule of life for believers. "Paul saw in the same law a curse upon those who did not *totally* obey (Gal. 3:10/Deut. 27:26)" [F.Dale Bruner, *A Theology of the Holy Spirit* [Eerdmans, 1970], p. 226].

This tension can be resolved only as we approach the law "in Christ." Our "rule" or canon, must begin with the redemption of Christ and the pervasive ethical demand which flows out of it. Christians, by marriage to Christ, have been released from the law, in order that they might bring forth fruit to God in newness of Spirit (Rom. 6:14). It is only as we come to grips with our not-under-law, but under-grace status in Christ that we can properly understand why sin no longer lords it over us (Rom. 6:14). It is only in this way that we can do full justice to *both* the absolute rigor of the law, and our freedom in the gospel from it. In the gospel we are *not*, as Watson suggests, justified without the law, and then sanctified by it. No, we are justified by faith in Christ, and then we live by faith in the Son of God. Is the believer then, in a "lawless" condition? Absolutely not. He is under the yoke of Christ (Matt.11:29-30); he is in-law to Christ (1 Cor. 9:21); he will fulfil the "law of Christ" (Gal. 6:2). Thus, as even Ernest Kevan admits, "grace is more commanding than law!" (*The Law of God In Christian Experience* [London,

1955], p. 66). If this be the case, why don't we just concentrate on *Christ*, on newness of life *in Him*, and the gracious demand that *He* makes on our living?

BUILT-IN FRUSTRATION

I suggest that Watson's ethical perspective brings with it built-in frustration. The believer is asked to learn the "hard lesson to live above the law, yet walk according to the law... to walk in the law in respect of duty, but to live above it in respect of comfort" (Samuel Bolton, *The True Bounds of Christian Freedom*. pp. 219-220). Marriage to Christ brings with it a new relationship; and in this relationship we are to derive our comfort, our duty, our everything *from Christ*— our Husband, our Bread of Life, our Vine, our Prophet.

If we focus on *anyone or anything* other than Christ we run the risk of missing *everything important*. And we must ask ourselves these questions: does the new commandment to love, as Christ loved us, leave us with nothing to do? Is there so little here that we must look elsewhere for a comprehensive ethical starting point? Why is it that in most books I have studied dealing with Christian ethics, virtually no attention is given to the infinite demand found in the new commandment? Why do we suppose that ethical fullness is found *only* in Exodus 20?

SERMON ON THE MOUNT

Perhaps the reply to the last question would be: because *our Lord* cited the Decalogue, as is evinced in His teachings on the Mount. Let us consider this observation for a moment. In Matt. 5:21-48 we find the Lord citing some of the Ten Commandments, and other commandments from the O.T.

This certainly indicates their ethical profitableness. However, what important fact clearly emerges at the conclusion of His teachings? The One who spoke all these words possessed "authority" (Matt. 7:28-29), and directed people, *in terms of a starting point*, to His sayings (Matt. 7:24,26). This substantiates the point I have previously made: Moses is approached *through Christ*, and, in terms of searching for a law-giver, we are directed by our Lord's own statements to Himself as the One having the words of eternal life (cf. John 6:68; Acts 3:22). All of this indicates that while Moses is not discarded as irrelevant, his "glory" cannot be compared to that of Christ (2 Cor. 3:7-11), and his writings were about the Son of God.

ROMANS 8:4

This brings us to another question. Is not the goal of redemption in Christ to see the "righteousness of the law" come to expression in our lives? Yes, but what exactly is the "righteousness of the law"? Paul could have easily stated that the goal was that the law might be fulfilled in us. But does the law not testify to a righteousness, to something beyond itself? "The law is therefore not so significant as the fundamental principles which it embodies" (Kaye, *Law and Morality,* p. 79). Are not the two great commandments found elsewhere than the Decalogue, but certainly in the O.T. (Lev. 19:18; Deut. 6:5)? Cannot Jesus summarily state that the whole law hangs on these two commandments, and that everything in the Law and Prophets can be comprehended in the broad principle of "however you would want others to treat you, do likewise to them" (Matt. 7:12; cf. Luke 6:31)?

And is not all this summed up in the single commandment to love? Our love to God and neighbor is now determined and conditioned by the act of God in sending Christ (John 3:16). We love because He first loved us in Christ (1 John 4:19). It is only with this perspective that we can understand how believers can actually perform a righteousness which "exceeds that of the Scribes and Pharisees" (Matt. 5:20). The law absolutely fails to bring righteous living; rather, it stirs up sin (Rom. 8:3; 7:8); it is only release from the law by marriage to Christ that the righteousness of the law can be fulfilled in those who walk in the Spirit (Rom. 6:14, 18; 8:4; Gal. 5:16, 18).

ENGLAND A "NEW ISRAEL"

Another significant belief that flows out of Watson's understanding of law is that he sees England as an "Israel." Thus he can justify the use of the sword in "standing for Christ": "In former times the nobles of Polonia, when the gospel was read, laid their hands upon their swords, signifying that they were ready to defend the faith, and hazard their lives for the gospel (p. 18). When discussing the blessing of being "delivered from places of idolatry" (p. 25), he rejoices in the "goodness of God to our nation [England], in bringing us out of mystic Egypt, delivering us from popery…Oh, what cause we have to bless God for delivering us from popery! It was a mercy to be delivered from the Spanish invasion and the powder treason; but it is far greater to be delivered from the popish religion, which would have made God give us a bill of divorce" (pp. 26-27). He conceives of God as being married to England (as God was a husband to Israel), and that the wrong state-religion would cause God to "divorce" Watson's homeland! "Pray", he goes on to say, "that the true Protestant religion may still flourish among us…O pray that the Lord will continue the visible token of his presence among us, his ordinances, that England may be called *Jehovah-shammah*, 'the Lord is there'" (pp. 28-29). This geographical conception of Christ's kingdom is a natural outcome of an unhealthy old covenant orientation, which points citizens and nations to the old exodus, instead of *starting* with the mighty spiritual exodus accomplished in Christ.

A pervasive Christ-orientation is missing in Watson's ethics. He says, "if the moral law could justify, what need was there of Christ's dying?" (p. 44). But he earlier stated that the moral law was *able* to "sanctify" (p. 13), so we must ask him, "If this be the case, what need is there of the Holy Spirit?" His system leaves us in an awkward (and impossible) situation where the law cannot justify, but it can sanctify. According to him, we need Christ to justify us; but the law is sufficient to instruct us. I think it is obvious that there is something very incongruous taking place here.

CONTEMPORARY REFORMED THOUGHT

Walter Chantry, *Today's Gospel: Authentic or Synthetic?*

A New Covenant orientation to Gospel preaching is found in *The First London Confession of Faith*, 1644. Here is an excerpt from it.

> That the tendency of the gospel to the conversion of sinners, is absolutely free, no way requiring, as absolutely necessary, any qualifications, preparations, terrors of the Law, or preceding Ministry of the Law, but only and alone the naked soul, as a sinner and ungodly to receive Christ, as crucified, dead, and buried, and risen again being made a Prince and a Savior for such sinners (Article XXV).

But in *Today's* Gospel, Walt Chantry posits that Law-preaching must come before Gospel presentation. His use of Scripture to establish this thesis is questionable. He uses 1 John 3:4 to assert "that there is a moral code which defines righteousness and sin. 'Sin is the transgression of the law' (p. 69; cf. p. 77). Literally, the Greek reads, "sin is lawlessness." The Greek word is *anomia*. It is a catch-word for all forms of wickedness.

It is arbitrary on Mr. Chantry's part to automatically link this word to an objective code, the Ten Commandments. For example, in Matt. 7:22-23, religious people claim "that they have prophesied, cast out devils and worked wonders "in His name." But Christ replies, "depart from Me, you who are working iniquity" (*anomian*). Is the wickedness mentioned here specifically related to the violation of some code? W. Gutbrod notes concerning the word *anomia:*

> In the New Testament *anomia* has the same range as else-where. In the plural (only in quotations), it means the simple *sinful* act; in this connection no thought is given to its association with the law as the yardstick by which the deed in question is shown to be sin…Service to sin leads to a general condition of *anomia*…Since Paul is speaking here [2 Cor. 6:14] to a…community which is not tied to the standard of the O.T. law, it is evident that here *anomia* does not derive its chief meaning from the O.T., but means simply sin, unrighteousness…[There is not in the use of anomia in 1 John 3:4] a reference to the O.T. law inherent in the word (*Law, Bible Key Words* from TDNT [London 1962], pp. 136, 137, 138).

1 John 3:4 is a crucial verse in Chantry's thought to establish that sin is conceived of in terms of violating the Ten

Commandments. But in looking at the word *anomia*, this is a tenuous position at best.

Rom. 3:20, "by the law is the knowledge of sin," is used by Mr. Chantry to prove that repentance "requires a use of the moral law to designate sin and holiness" (p. 70). While the Ten Commandments are a part of "the law," Paul here in this context means the *whole Old Testament* by the word "law" (cf. John Murray, *Romans,* Vol.1, pp. 240, 105). Chantry says, "this moral law comes 'that every mouth may be stopped, and all the world become guilty before God'" (p. 70). But in one of the longest quotations from the Old Testament, Paul cited nothing from the *Ten Commandments*, but quoted from the Psalms and Isaiah (vv. 10-18). The "law" here cannot be equated with the *Ten Commandments*, which Chantry mistakenly does.

On p. 72 Chantry presents the Reformed perspective on the law in the believer's life: in justification he is no longer under the condemnation of the law, but in sanctification he is under the law as a guide. Paul, however, teaches that the believer is not "under law" in *sanctification* (Rom. 6:14-15). One must be "under grace" in order for the non-dominion of sin to be a reality in their life. Chantry suggests that "nothing but the moral law can define for us what sanctified behavior is" (p.72). This is simply not true. The writers of the New Testament feel at ease referencing holy behavior to the person and work of Jesus Christ (Phil. 2:5; Rom. 15:3; 2 Cor. 8:9, 1 John 3:16; 4:10-11; 1 Pet. 2:21-23). As Robert D. Brinsmead puts it so beautifully:

> Paul virtually never appeals to the law—"Thou shalt not." When he demands certain behavior of the church, he appeals to the holy history of Christ, into which the

church is incorporated, and from that standpoint then makes his ethical appeal (*Judged By The Gospel*, p. 213).

This does not mean that Exodus 20 is worthless, but it does radically qualify the dogmatic assertion of Mr. Chantry that *nothing* but the "moral law" can define holy behavior.

Mr. Chantry uses John 16:8 as proof that "in the task of bringing men into the kingdom, the moral law and the gospel are the two major instruments in the arsenal of the Spirit" (p. 90). However, there is nothing in the text to indicate that the Spirit will take the law and convince people of their sin. Rather, all three elements of conviction are Christ-centered: "it should not be overlooked that all the three aspects of the work of the Holy Spirit dealt with in these verses are interpreted Christologically. Sin, righteousness and judgment are all to be understood because of the way in which they relate to Christ" (Leon Morris, *Commentary on the Gospel of John*, p. 699). There is no example in the Book of Acts where any part of the Decalogue was preached in order to convict the audience of sin. Rather the O.T. was used to preach Christ.

Thus James Buchanan in his book on the Holy Spirit states in regard to John 16:8-11: "It may be safely affirmed that it is by the Spirit's witness to Christ that he first brought to see the magnitude of his guilt…Christ's exaltation…is *sufficient*…to carry home conviction of sin" (p. 64, emphasis mine).

Mr. Chantry believes that under the new covenant "an entire day is to be kept holy unto God…Only a seventh part of their time is claimed by the Lord for special worship" (p. 133). I suggest that such a perspective does injustice to the passing away of "the rudiments of the world" (Gal. 4:3; Col. 2:8, 20). In John 4:20-24 Jesus teaches that the era when special temporal considerations are in force is past. We no longer come to a temple, our bodies are a temple of the Holy Spirit (1 Cor. 6:19). We do not come to the "house of God" (a building); the congregation is the house of God (1 Cor. 3:10; Eph. 2:21). We do not keep a Sabbath day; we enjoy the rest of the Sabbath reality, Jesus Christ (Col. 2:16-17). We do not view a seventh of our time as special, all of our time belongs to the Lord (Eph. 5:16; Rom. 14:8).

Palestine is no more a "holy land" than the deserts in Barstow, California where I was born. Sunday is no holier than Saturday—unless someone personally wishes to regard a day to the Lord (Rom. 14:5-6). The December Christmas season is not holy. Buildings are not holy. Infants of believers are not "covenantally holy." There are no holy cities or nations. The water in baptism, and the bread and the wine in the Lord's Supper are not holy, even though Luther said they were (*Martin Luther:* Selected *Writings*, John Dillenberger [Doubleday, 1961], pp. 229-233). The believer is dead to the rudiments of the world (Col. 2:20) so that he can serve his neighbor in love (Gal. 5:13). Is it not the case that many dear people are hung-up on things like "touch not, taste not, handle not" (Col. 2:21)?

A CHANGED PERSPECTIVE: ROBERT D. BRINSMEAD

Judged By the Gospel: A Review of Adventism

"The Gospel and Ethics" (pp. 203-253)

RDB submits that recapturing the gospel will lead us to "An Ethic of Grateful Celebration," "An Ethic of Faith and Love," "An Ethic of Freedom and Responsibility," and "An

Ethic of Forgiveness." I regard this section as the high point of the book. My heart was absolutely thrilled by "An Ethic of Grateful Celebration."

In many cases the Bible is approached as "a rule book on human behavior" (p. 207). Proof-texts are isolated to prove "non-drinking, non-smoking, no jewelry wearing, vegetarianism (or at least no pork eating), tithe paying, Sabbath keeping and church organization" (p. 207). But "the Bible has no independent interest in ethics...The Bible is written as history. It is the story of God's redemptive acts. Biblical ethics are not artificially attached to this story. They are embedded in the story itself...When biblical ethics are removed from the context of redemptive history, they cease to be biblical ethics...As far as the Bible is concerned, ethics have no independent value and no meaning outside of the saving deeds of God" (p. 209).

RDB shows that the Exodus event was the central redemptive act for Israel, and out of that event came the ethical demand upon the covenant people (pp. 209-211): "[redemptive act:] I am the Lord your God who brought you out of the land of Egypt, out of the house of bondage. [Moral imperative:] You shall have no other gods before Me" (Exod. 20:2-3). The Red Sea deliverance was not an end in itself. It was *a type of the future exodus to be carried out in the death, burial, and resurrection of Christ.* Thus the reference point for life in Christ is not the shadow, *but the saving work of Christ,* with pointed focus on Golgotha: "God's final act in Christ refracts the covenantal order of life to us" (p. 212). Hence, our obedience is carried out in grateful celebration of the redemptive act that secured our freedom (John 5:12-13; Gal. 5:1).

"[Paul's] appeals on how to live are made on the basis of what God has done for us in Christ. It is in view of God's gospel mercies that we are to present our lives as a living sacrifice to God (Rom. 12:1-3)…Paul virtually never appeals to the law—'Thou shalt not.' When he demands certain behavior of the church, he appeals to the holy history of Christ…and from that standpoint then makes his ethical appeal" (p. 213).

Ethic of Guilt

RDB makes a very significant point by observing that if our behavior is not a grateful reaction to Christ's manifestation in history for us and in us, we run the risk of falling into "an ethic of guilt" (p. 214). Listen to these powerful words:

> I fear that far too much Adventism is an ethic of guilt. People are motivated by guilt to keep the Sabbath, to pay tithe, to be loyal to the denomination, to eat the right food, to eschew jewelry, to avoid worldly amusements… the motivation of guilt will produce results…The Pauline Epistles do not present a motivation of guilt but a motivation of grace. Unless a religious group gives free course to the gospel, and unless its pulpits ring with the liberating proclamation of grace, the religious group will become a religious slave camp…The greatest instrument of coercion in traditional Adventism is guilt. The two greatest motivational forces in the world are guilt and grace. Where the gospel is not paramount, guilt is the instrument by which we motivate ourselves and others… Guilt will drive a missionary to compass land and sea to make a single convert. Rome has learned to harness the power of guilt… Rome has always complained that justification by faith alone always severs the nerve of the moral imperative. But she is really concerned with people who are no longer guilty and can therefore no longer be manipulated. If the Adventist

community does not live by the gospel, it is guilt which makes people keep the Sabbath, pay tithe…Sermons which exhort people to conform to certain behavior are generally intended to make people guilty enough to elicit the desired response (pp. 214-215, 291-292).

The Gospel walk is not a guilt-trip; it is a walk of faith and freedom because God has fully forgiven us for the sake of His Son. He remembers our sins no more. People captured by the consciousness of their freedom in Christ cannot be manipulated. This is what religious establishments fear most: justified people, no longer in bondage to the elemental spirits, but constrained by the love of Christ (Col. 2:8; 2 Cor. 5: 14-15).

The Reformation View of the Church

I believe RDB's presentation of the Reformation idea of the church (pp. 267-270) fails to give the full picture. For example, he says that "Luther had no faith in political intrigue, in military might or in the aid of civil power" (p. 197). Luther may have said that on paper, but as time elapsed, his ministry revealed capitulation to the German princes (cf. Kurt Aland, *Four Reformers* [Augsburg Pub. House, 1979], pp. 30, 48, Leonard Verduin, *The Reformers and Their Stepchildren*, pp. 18-19). The whole Reformation movement was connected to the ungodly union of church and state, and thus to "the use of the sword against the godless" (Aland p. 39). This fact *had catastrophic effects on the Reformation view of the church.*

Again, RDB states that "with the Reformers the church was essentially a community" (p. 269). I cannot agree with this. Because of the territorial conception of the church that emerged everywhere the Reformation spread, it was impossible for the community dimension to be a reality. How could it be when the boundaries of the "church" coincided with the boundaries of the state? It was among the Anabaptists that the church as a separate believing community was realized. For Zwingli, Luther and Calvin to opt for a believer's church, separate from the civil domain, would have required them to repudiate twelve centuries of tradition since Constantine (Verduin p. 19). This they did not do, and for this reason the Anabaptists were a persecuted people. The Reformation carried on the territorial conception of the church perpetrated by Catholicism—they only put Lutheranism or Calvinism in the saddle instead of the Pope (Verduin p. 36). RDB should have had a chapter entitled "The Anabaptist view of the church."

Again, RDB says that Luther restored the idea of the servant nature of the church. It was no longer to be "the proud, triumphalistic church which demanded submission, but a poor, suffering church which wielded no power but the power of the gospel" (p. 269). Wrong again. It was the Anabaptists who captured the suffering nature of the church, not the Reformers. How could those who sided with the power of the sword to enforce a state religion maintain the stance of a "servant" church? As the Reformation blossomed, the Anabaptists pleaded with Luther to begin a believer's church, but to no avail. A state church cannot be a *suffering* church, for it rests on the arm of the sword; a state cannot be a servant church, for it must resort to coercion and fear (cf. Lord Acton, "The Protestant Theory of Persecution," *Essays on Freedom and Power* [World pub. Co. 1948), pp. 113-140).

Finally, RDB says that the Protestant Reformation resulted in "the triumph of the priesthood of all believers over the religious hierarchy" (p. 293). Yes and no. Certainly, the priesthood was restored in some important ways. "But they [the Reformers] retained a modified version of the clerical system of ministry in the church" (Robert Girard, *Brethren, Hang Together*, p. 127). The vision of the priesthood which emerged in the Reformation was essentially *individualistic not corporate*. That is, they emphasized that each believer has direct access to Christ and the Scriptures, and did not need intermediaries. However, the New Testament presentation of the priesthood relates primarily to the functioning of the priests in their mutual relationships with one another. The focus on the "minister" in Protestant churches in many ways took the place of the focus on the "priest" in Catholicism. Thus, in mainline Protestantism, the priesthood of believers still ended up being stifled by some presence of authority figures.

RDB notes that "Luther declared that all believers alike have the authority to preach, baptize, administer the Supper and judge doctrine" (p. 269). That sounds good on paper, but where did he ever allow these things to be practiced? It was the Anabaptists who carried out such ideas to the chagrin of the state-church authorities. And what poor believer would have the courage to question the "Doctors," especially if civil punishment might be his portion for taking issue with the state religion? ■

58 TO 0: HOW CHRIST LEADS THROUGH THE ONE ANOTHERS

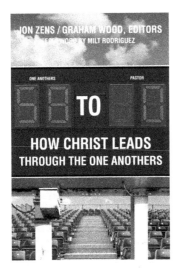

There have been thousands of books published about the aspects of church leadership, but comparatively very little time has been spent on the necessity of the church to "love one another," and all the rest of the one anothers that flow out of Christ's new command. Based on observations since 1965, Jon Zens' conclusion is that we need more and more of Christ, and less and less of the traditional views of "leadership." This book sets forth the Jesus-centered way of functioning as brothers and sisters in the Body of Christ...Contributors span from 1937 - 2013: Hans van Campenhausen, Judy Schindler, Bruce Davidson, Daryl Erkel, Matthew and Christa McKirland, Hendrik Hart, Russ Ross, Lawrence Burkholder, R.L. Wysong, Norbert Ward, Katt Huff, Stephen Crosby, Fydor Dosteyevsky, H.L. Mencken, John Howard Yoder, and Frank Viola. These authors take issue with the traditional understandings of church life, and point the way to Christ, the only rightful Leader of the ekklesia.

THE LIFE OF CHRIST IN THE EARLY CHURCH: WHERE WERE THE WRITTEN SCRIPTURES?

JON ZENS

[This is the essence of a presentation given to an assembly in Gainesville, Florida, January, 2012.]

Without question, many of the points I will make today have been stated well by others. But it is possible that as the Lord has worked in me—especially in the past year—that I will be putting a number of pieces together in a way that will be striking and gripping to your hearts. I pray that you will be impressed by the fact that when we speak of "renewal" in the Body of Christ, it is clearly not a question of uncovering something that has been missing, but rather a matter of unleashing Christ in us, who is already there!

I have a request to make of you. I know it is impossible for us to do this in actuality, but please try to use your imagination and transport yourself into a First Century gathering of saints. There you are, most likely in the home of a more well-to-do family or brother/sister. You are surrounded by people who have come out of the town synagogue and the pagan culture—Jews and Gentiles, now part of the New Humanity Jesus created by his death and resurrection. Back then there were no church buildings, no ordained-clergy, no hymn books, no pulpit, and most notably for our purposes today—*no Bible.*

Let's step back for a moment and think about what led up to Christ expressing himself in unbelievable ways through *ekklesias* all over the known-world during the period of AD 30-70. How did the Body of Christ function in this admittedly glorious blossoming of his presence on earth?

In John 14-16 Jesus revealed to his disciples that he would be exiting the earth and returning to the Father. But he promised that he would not leave them as orphans. After his leaving he would send the Holy Spirit to dwell in them. Jesus specifically noted that the sending of the Spirit would be a *coming of himself*—"I am coming to you" (John 14:18). This was fulfilled on the Day of Pentecost—"He [Jesus] has poured out this which you see and hear" (Acts 2:33). Thus, *the coming of the Spirit on the Day of Pentecost was in fact the coming of Christ to dwell in his Bride.*

What was the social make-up of those coming into Messiah's community? The gap between the few wealthy and many poor was very wide. Most people in the First Century would be considered "lower class." For sure, there was a 94% illiteracy rate in Jesus' day—even in Judaism. As James D.G.

Dunn points out, "the probability is that the great majority of Galileans, including the great majority of those who followed Jesus, were technically illiterate" (*Jesus, Paul & the Gospels*, p. 9; cf. p. 22). When Peter and John were hauled before the Jewish officials, isn't it remarkable that these leaders were astonished because "these two are unlettered and without expertise," and "they recognized that Peter and John had been with Jesus" (Acts 4:13).

Thus the society surrounding the early church was an *oral culture*. It is imperative for us to fully realize that the first believers carried out their new lives in Christ *with no Bible*. The brothers and sisters did not have American Bible Society New Testaments tucked in the pockets of their attire! "For five centuries," Dunn notes, "we have been accustomed to the benefits of printing. Our minds are print-dominated. We have a literary mind-set. We think in terms of information typically conveyed in writing and by reading. We think more naturally of the reader reading as an individual than of the audience learning only by what it hears" (*Jesus, Paul & the Gospels*, p. 9).

How, then, did the earliest brothers and sisters function without any written documents? Exactly as Christ did—by hearing from Father and following his leading. Listen to Jesus' own words about how he lived each day:

> There is a judge for the one who rejects me and does not accept my words; that very word which I spoke will condemn him on the last day. For I did not speak of my own accord, but the Father who sent me commanded me what to say and how to say it. I know that his command leads to eternal life. So whatever I say is just what the Father has told me to say (12:47-50)…Don't you believe that I am in

the Father, and that the Father is in me? The words I say to you are not just my own. Rather, it is the Father living in me who is doing his work...If you love me, you will do what I command (14:10,15)...Jesus replied, If anyone loves me, he will obey my teaching. My Father will love him, and we will come to him and make our home with him. He who does not love me will not obey my teaching. These words you hear are not my own; they belong to the Father who sent me (14:23-24)...I have revealed you to those whom you gave me out of the world. They were yours; you gave them to me and they have obeyed your word. Now they know that everything you have given me comes from you. For I gave them the words you gave me and they accepted them (17:6-8).

We can see a basic pattern from these words as to how Christ lived out his short life on earth: *listening to Father, hearing Father, seeing (perceiving) what Father is saying, speaking as he gives utterance, and doing his bidding.* As the Father was to Christ, so Christ is now to us. We listen to and hear from Christ which results in revelation (seeing), and then we speak and do his pleasure.

The early believers had no Bible, but they had that which was most important—Christ in them by the Holy Spirit. Can you contemplate living your daily life in Christ without a Bible? Yet that was the reality in the First Century when it cannot be denied that the most unprecedented growth and expression in the *ekklesias* occurred.

Without any Bibles, what would a group of believers in the First Century share and talk about with each other? The answer is simple—*Christ!* Recall John's amazing summary remarks about what our Lord did on while on earth: "And many other signs indeed did Jesus in the presence of his disciples, which are not written in this book...And there are also many other things which Jesus did, which if every one of them was written down, I would imagine that even the world itself could not contain the books that would need to be written" (John 20:30; 21:25).

James Dunn comments on the development of how Jesus came to be the "talk of the town," so to speak:

> Jesus' teaching was given *orally*; it began orally...We can safely assume that the news about Jesus was initially passed around *orally*. The stories about Jesus would no doubt have been the subject of many a conversation in bazaars and around campfires. The disciples of Jesus no doubt spoke about what they had seen Jesus do, and about his teaching. This would have been the beginning of the Jesus tradition. It would be celebrated and meditated on in groups of his followers in oral terms (*Jesus, Paul & the Gospels*, p. 23).

In light of the vast, infinite person of Christ unveiled in Colossians 1:13-20, and the inexhaustible life that he fulfilled on earth, how could the saints ever run out of praise, adoration—and any other type of content—concerning their dear Savior, Redeemer and Husband? Also, of course, there were believers who came from synagogue backgrounds who could talk about Jesus from what they had heard every Sabbath from Moses and the prophets.

Here is an important fact that few have pondered: The first letter from Paul to an *ekklesia* occurred around AD 49—the book of Galatians. That's about nineteen years after the Day of Pentecost. Look at all the wondrous work the Lord did in building his *ekklesias* for about twenty years without any New Covenant writings! Of course, problems surfaced as time elapsed and letters were written to respond to the needs. These were read to an assembly, and perhaps passed on to other *ekklesias*.

Have you ever thought about the fact that there were very likely *ekklesias* that never received a letter from an apostle, and may have never, or rarely, heard epistles to other groups read to them?

How much of what we call the "New Testament" did believers living in AD 65 ever hear read aloud in a gathering, or hear about from other saints? Is it not highly probable that a majority of Christ-followers between the years AD 50 to AD 70 had never heard of or knew about many of the twenty-seven writings we designate as the "New Testament"?

Let's consider one huge implication that flows out of the previous paragraph. 1 Timothy was written around AD 62-63. This letter was written to a specific person, not an assembly. Obviously, Timothy would then process Paul's concerns with reference to the *ekklesia* in Ephesus. Now how many believers between AD 62 to AD 100 would have even known about the existence of 1 Timothy 2:11-12—verses that in subsequent post-apostolic times were used to marginalize women? We perhaps assume that the entire early church was somewhat familiar with the "New Testament" writings, but that simply was not the case.

WHERE WERE THE WRITTEN DOCUMENTS?

Until AD 49-50 the only written scriptures were the scrolls of the "Old Testament." These scrolls were kept in the synagogues and controlled by the Jewish hierarchy. The Jewish rank-and-file knew of Moses, the Psalms and the Prophets *orally*. "Their knowledge of the Torah did not come from

personal copies which each had, as would be the case today…
For the great majority, Torah knowledge came from hearing
it read to them by the minority who could read, Sabbath by
Sabbath in the synagogue" (Dunn, *Jesus, Paul & the Gospels*,
p. 23).

A rare exception can be seen in Acts 8:26-35. The
Ethiopian eunuch was returning home from Jerusalem, and
was reading out loud from scrolls of Isaiah. He, as the trea-
surer for Kandake, was a wealthy man and was somehow able
to purchase all or part of Isaiah. But such a luxury was far out
of reach for the average person.

It is very possible that all of the New Testament was
written before the fall of Jerusalem in AD 70 (cf. John A.T.
Robinson, *Redating the New Testament*, Wipf & Stock, 2001,
384 pp.).

From roughly AD 250 onwards copies of the NT documents were in the hands of the bishops and the developing
church hierarchy that became the Roman Catholic Church.
Just as in First Century Judaism when the OT scrolls were
controlled by the synagogue leaders, so in post-apostolic
times the NT documents were controlled by the clergy. In
both contexts the "laypeople" had virtually no access to the
written documents.

Jerome translated the Bible into Latin in the late Fourth
Century. This translation was "the Bible" until the 1500's.
Illiteracy was still very high, of course, from AD 400 to AD
1500, so the scriptures still were in the possession of the
church hierarchy.

With the invention of the printing press, however, the
Bible began to be translated into other languages. Luther
did a German translation. Wycliffe and Tyndale did English

translations. It became increasingly possible for the common people to read the Scriptures for themselves.

CONCLUDING THOUGHTS

One New Testament scholar, Carl Cosaert, makes the claim that "the early church was a 'text' driven religion and that fact should be noted" ("The Reliability of the New Testament Scriptures," Part 2, *Ministry*, November, 2011, p. 23). In light of our survey of certain First Century realities in the early church period of AD 30-70, I do not understand how he can make that claim. As far as I can tell, the early church was *Christ*-driven. It was the indwelling life of Christ in believers that accounts for the vibrancy of the first generation saints. In 2 Corinthians 3, Paul affirms that believers are the living letters that are "known and read by all people…having been inscribed not with ink, but by the Spirit of the living God; not in stone tablets, but in fleshy tablets of beating hearts" (vv. 2-3).

It has long been the case that outward Christianity was identified as a "religion of the Book." But that was certainly not the case in the First Century. Can we begin to grasp the fact that during the period of AD 30-70 when Christ's *ekklesias* burst into life all over the Roman Empire, the only explanation for their unparalleled vitality was that Christ's life-giving ministry by the Spirit was continuing through his Body on earth, not that they were glued to "the Bible"— which simply did not exist at that time. Lloyd Gardner notes in this regard:

> With this explosive beginning to the church, one hears no mention of several things. There was no church building, no pastor, no organized meetings, no worship team, no

sermons and no statements of doctrine, no evangelism programs, bulletins or order of worship… They were walking together in the glorious light of the resurrected Christ who was alive in them and in their midst (*The Heresy of Diotrephes*, Eleizer Call Ministries, 2007, pp. 168-169). ∎

For further reflection:

1. Raymond E. Brown, *The Churches the Apostles Left Behind*, Paulist Press, 1984, 156 pp.

2. Robert B. Coote & Mary P. Coote, *Power, Politics, and the Making of the Bible: An Introduction*, Fortress Press, 1990, 191 pp.

3. Carl P. Cosaert, "The Reliability of the New Testament Scriptures: Earliest Manuscript Evidence," Part 1, *Ministry*, September, 2011, pp. 6-9; "The Reliability of the New Testament Scriptures: Early Christians & the Codex," Part 2, *Ministry*, November, 2011, pp. 21-24.

4. David L. Dungan, *Constantine's Bible: Politics & the Making of the New Testament*, SCM Press, 2006, 224 pp.

5. James D.G. Dunn, *Jesus, Paul, and the Gospels*, Eerdmans, 2011, especially pages 8-22.

6. Philip F. Esler, ed., *Modelling Early Christianity: Social-Scientific Studies of the New Testament in Its Context*, Routledge, 1995, 349 pp.

7. Philip Jenkins, *Jesus Wars: How Four Patriarchs, Three Queens, and Two Emperors Decided What Christians Would Believe for the Next 1,500 Years*, HarperOne, 2010, 328 pp.

8. Bruce Malina & Richard Rohrbaugh, *Social-Science Commentary on the Synoptic Gospels*, Fortress Press, 1992, 422 pp.

9. Dennis Mulkey, *Treason Against Christ: A Summons to Reclaim the Authentic Identity of the Word of God*, Tate Publishing, 2012, 305 pp.

10. Carolyn Osiek & David L. Balch, *Families in the New Testament World: Households & House Churches*, Westminster/John Knox, 1997, 329 pp.

11. J.S. Riggs, "Canon of the New Testament," *The International Standard Bible Encyclopedia*, James Orr, ed., Eerdmans, 1976, Vol. I, pp. 563-566.

12. George L. Robinson, "Canon of the Old Testament," *The International Standard Bible Encyclopedia*, James Orr, ed., Eerdmans, 1976, Vol. I, pp. 554-563.

13. Christian Smith, *The Bible Made Impossible: Why Biblicism Is Not A Truly Evangelical Reading of Scripture*, Brazos Press, 2011, 220 pp.

14. Jakob Van Bruggen, "Bible Translating to 1637," *The Future of the Bible*, Thomas Nelson, 1978, pp. 37-54.

15. Frank Viola, *The Untold Story of the New Testament*, Destiny Image.

16. John H. Walton/D. Brent Sandy, *The Lost World of Scripture*, IVP, 2013, 320 pp. Ancient Near Eastern societies were "hearing dominant" and had nothing comparable to modern books or authors.

17. John H. Yoder, "Church Growth Issues in Theological Perspective," *The Challenge of Church Growth: A Symposium*, William R. Shenk, ed., Institute of Mennonite Studies, 1973, pp. 25-47.

18. John H. Yoder, "The One or the Many? The Pauline Vision & the Rest of the Reformation," *Servants of the Word: Ministry in the Believers Churches*, David B. Eller, ed., Brethren Press, 1990, pp. 51-64.

19. Jon Zens, "The Life of Christ in the Early Church: They Had No Scrolls in Their Laps," audio, www.searchingtogether.org/media/audio/ChristsLifeNoBible_JZ_Gainesville_FL_01-12.mp3

GATHERINGS IN THE EARLY CHURCH:SHARING CHRIST WITH ONE ANOTHER...NOT LISTENING TO A PULPIT MONOLOGUE

WILLIAM BARCLAY (WITH COMMENTS BY JON ZENS, 1981)

[Although I have problems with some of William Barclay's views, the following observations on Paul's teaching in 1 Corinthians 14, taken from his The Letters to the Corinthians *(Westminster Press, 1st Edition, 1956, pp. 149-150), may be the best concise summary of the spirit of early church meetings that I have ever seen. I have added headings that are not in the original text, and will make several comments after Barclay's excerpts.]*

LIBERTY, BUT NOT DISORDER

Paul comes near to the end of this section with some very practical advice. He is determined that anyone who possesses a gift should receive every chance to exercise that gift: but he is equally determined that the services of the Church should not thereby become a kind of competitive disorder. Only two or three are to exercise the gift of tongues, and then only if there is someone there to interpret. All have the gift of forth-telling truth. but again only two or three are to exercise it; and if someone in the congregation has the conviction that he has received a special message, the person who is speaking must give way to him and give him the opportunity to express it. The person who is speaking can perfectly well do so, and need not say that he is carried away by inspiration and cannot stop, because the preacher IS able to control his own spirit. There must be liberty but there must be no disorder. The God of peace must be worshipped in peace.

THE SAINTS' GATHERING: *FREEDOM WITHIN STRUCTURE*

It is true to say that there is no more interesting section in the whole letter than this, for it sheds a flood of light on what a Church service was like in the early Church. There was obviously a freedom and an informality about it which is completely strange to our ideas.

A "PASTOR" IS NOT THE ONLY SOURCE OF EDIFICATION

Clearly the early Church had no professional ministry. True, the apostles stood out with a very special authority: but at this stage the Church had no professional local ministry. It was open to anyone who had a gift to use that gift. Has the Church done rightly or wrongly in instituting a professional ministry? Clearly there is something essential in that, in our busy age when people are so preoccupied with material things, one should be set apart to live close to God and to bring his fellows the truth and the guidance and the comfort which God gives to him. But on the other hand there is the obvious danger that when a person becomes a professional preacher he is at least sometimes in the position of having to say something when he really has nothing to say. However that may be, it must remain true that if one has a message to give others no ecclesiastical rules and regulations should be able to stop him from giving it. It is certainly a mistake to think that only the professional ministry can ever bring God's truth to others.

THE PRIESTHOOD PREPARED TO FUNCTION

There was obviously flexibility about the order of service in the Early Church which is now totally lacking. There was clearly no settled order at all. Everything was informal enough to allow any one who felt that he had a message to give to give it. It may well be that we set far too much store on dignity and order nowadays. It may well be that we have become the slaves of orders of service. The really notable thing about an early Church service must have been that almost everyone came with a sense that they had both the privilege and the obligation of contributing something to it. A person did not come with the sole intention of being a passive listener. He did not come only to receive, he came also to give. Obviously this had its dangers for it is clear that in Corinth there were those who were too fond of the sound of their own voices: but nonetheless the Church must have been in those days much more the real possession of the ordinary Christian. It may well be that the Church lost something when she delegated so much to the professional ministry and left so little to the ordinary Church member; and it may well be that the blame lies not with the ministry for annexing those rights, but with the laity for abandoning them, because it is all too true that there are many Church members whose attitude is that they think far more of what the Church can do for them than of what they can do for the Church and who are very ready to criticize what is done but very unready to take any share in doing the Church's work themselves.

COMMENTS ON BARCLAY'S REMARKS

Barclay's statement that in our "busy age" it is good to have "one set apart to live close to God and to bring his fellows the truth and the guidance and the comfort which God gives to him" lacks Scriptural support. There is certainly nothing wrong with an Elder receiving financial help from the church, but such support is by no means limited to "one person." It would be good for the church, depending on available resources, to help as many elders as possible. But such support has nothing to do with "busy times," or some special "Pastor" status. It is simply a means to relieve the Elders (plural) from the need to produce an income so that they can be free to spend more time ministering to the needs of the church (Greg Hufstetler, "The Support of Elders in the NT," *Searching Together*, 7:2, 1978, pp. 46-50).The fact is that there is no similarity between the description and function of the Elders in the NT and the "professional ministry" that appeared later in the history of the church.

Some argue that 1 Cor. 14 must be "qualified" by later NT revelation. Al Martin, for example, alleges that "churches are taking on their more permanent form under the direction of

Timothy and Titus and you see a transition. The directions of Paul with regard to the life of the church at Corinth are materially different from the directions in the Pastoral Epistles." ("Law and Gospel," message given in Toronto, February 11, 1980). Just what is "materially different"? Is I Cor. 14 in some way at variance with 1 & 2 Timothy and Titus? Of course not! Nothing about elders is mentioned in the Corinthian church. The NT letters were written to the *assemblies*, not to "leaders." Thus, we must conclude that there is *nothing* incompatible between 1 Cor. 14 and later NT revelation. The idea that as time went on the early church gatherings saw an *increasing* focus on the ministry of elders and a corresponding *decrease* in the ministry of the general priesthood is without Biblical foundation. The *full* ministry of elders is completely compatible with the *full* functioning of the priesthood. But post-apostolic church life quickly moved away from the simplicity of NT polity to a position where the church hierarchy swallowed up the ministry of the spiritual priesthood.

As I have studied this issue, I have observed that a good many commentators generally agree on the freedom-within-structure nature of the NT church gatherings. Consider, for example, the following comments on "let everyone be quick to hear, slow to speak and slow to anger" (James 1:19). Curtis Vaughn observed:

> There may be an illusion to the free and unstructured worship of early Christian assemblies *(James: A Study Guide.* Zondervan. 1960. p. 35).

Similarly. Earl Kelly noted:

> It is possible that contentious Christian babes were taking advantage of the informal style of worship in the early Christian church to produce wrangling *(James: A*

Primer for Christian Living, Presbyterian & Reformed. 1974. p. 69).

This begs the question: if it is acknowledged widely that such structured informality existed in the early church meetings, on what basis do we *no longer* practice the basic revelation found in I Cor. 14? Why was *it good* for them, but apparently *unworkable* or *dangerous* for us? Must we not also ask whether the traditional order of service that is so widely adopted today faithfully reflects such structured informality, or is it instead a closed formality that effectively stifles the intended "one-another" ministry of the gathered "priesthood of believers"? There is nothing in the NT about having a "church service," as we know it, in any case. ■

COMMENTS

I ordered some of your materials back in January, I think it was and wanted to get back to you right away as we were so blessed with all that you shared. However the time has slipped away but in the meantime we have read and re read the books and watched and shared the video's. We have the weekend video series as well as What's with Paul and Women, Church Every 1/2 Mile and a few other titles which have been incredibly useful in helping us find our way.

You have brought so much clarity to the whole concept of body life and "church." I found it particularly helpful to understand the difference between old and new covenant theology and to see how Dispensationalism has been detrimental in rightly dividing the scriptures.

Although I have been a believer for 40 years. I feel like I am relearning everything, and this time with far more joy than ever before. The pages of the Bible are opening up for me like never before in my life. We have recently started meeting with a small group of believers outside of the "traditional church," and again your works have been so helpful.

We are in the process of relieving ourselves of the old way of seeing things and looking for Christ alone to be our head in all things. Thank you for your diligence in sharing all that God has given you. Your labor is definitely not vain in the Lord.

– Leah Hope

Jon, just wanted to say how much I enjoyed your article. "What about the word kephale in the New Testament?" Very interesting and thought provoking. You are ever the advocate for equality among all. I really appreciate that. Yours is a voice that needs to be heard! Love ya, bro!

– Pam Frazier

I can't begin to tell you how I have been blessed and encouraged by your ministry over the past 35 years! I continue to look forward to every issue you publish. May our glorious Lord continue to bless all that you do.

– Jerry Rasmus

Thank you Frank Viola, Milt and Mary Rodriguez, Jon Zens, Alan and Amy Jean Levine, for laying down your lives time and time again so that Christ can be head of his church on the earth and being expressed. For teaching by not mere word but in action the confidence we can have in knowing our Lord and living by his life. One person's decisions for Christ can affect a multitude of people, and that is evident with the expression of Christ on the earth today. And, lastly, for pointing us to him not yourselves. Never leaving a fingerprint behind so that truly he receives all the glory. Praise the Lord for your lives and faithfulness to the gospel of our Lord Jesus Christ.

— A Sister in Florida

Truly a great time with the body of Christ today! So glad Jon Zens could be with us. We are sooo sooooo blessed by all the wonderful things God is doing in our midst. The meeting was really great! Your teachings on the "Living Waters" is incredible. I hope that everyone can hear that inspiring message! It is an eye-opener! We are so blessed by it. Thanks for sharing the message about the living waters....that was so awesome! You will have to write a book on that now. I can't wait to hear it again. You laid a powerful foundation, it painted a huge picture that many need to see which will help people understand the true purpose of the Ekklesia and how we are to gather.

— Jayne Otterson

I am extremely thankful for brothers like you, Frank and all the others who have given language, to communicate the convictions of the heart, of the body of Christ. When I first came back, I have been advocating for organic meetings. I would leave a copy of Frank's book "Reimagining Church" on the coffee table. Any way, The lord used your Searching Together on Thomas Campbell and the early restoration movement to help me see that I should ease back a little and be faithful to the community God's given me, and check my heart a little. As I did this God started working on the hearts of some of my house- mates, and they started seeing that the meetings were getting dry and that we were not acting like a multifaceted body, but instead a top heavy bible study. After awhile, a brother stepped down from facilitating the meeting. And with no planning and no prep whatsoever we had our first, what I considered an authentic NewTestament style meeting. Everyone participated. It was the closest meeting I have been in to see 1 Cor. 14:26 in action. No person led it and everyone participated. It moved from prayer to songs to spontaneous teaching, but the cool thing was that it was all related to what everyone else was saying. It went for hours and no one took over; it was completely spontaneous, yet orderly. My whole house was blown away. Jesus was there and he was teaching us what it looked like to gather as an ekklesia. The next week we met at another brother's house and it was back to the same old same old, but this time people saw it for what it was and longed for the kind of meeting we had the previous week. This is where we are at as a community right now. I believe God is going to grant us more of these meetings, I believe.

– Mickey Sweet

Hey, Jon, I just want to`say 'I love you, brother!' I love your stuff. You have the best information in the Christian world as far as I'm concerned. It gets to the point and tells the truth. It doesn't play around with a lot of nonsense, and I appreciate it. I love you and pray for you. Thanks for the great work you do. You guys are the best. Searching Together ought to be in everybody's library.

– Danny Griffen

MORE FROM JON ZENS

- Dispensationalism: An Inquiry Into Its Leading Figures & Features, 1978

- Desiring Unity...Finding Division: Lessons from the 19th Century Restoration Movement, 1986

- Moses In the Millennium: An Analysis of Christian Reconstructionism, 1988

- This Is My Beloved Son, Hear Him: The Foundation of New Covenant Ethics & Ecclesiology, 1997

- A Church Building Every 1/2 Mile: What Makes American Christianity Tick? 2008

- What's With Paul & Women? Unlocking the Cultural Background to 1 Timothy 2, 2011

- No Will of My Own: How Patriarchy Smothers Female Dignity & Personhood, 2011

- Christ Minimized? A Response to Rob Bell's Love Wins, 2012

- The Pastor Has No Clothes: Moving from Clergy-Centered Church to Christ-Centered Ekklesia, 2012

- To Preach or Not to Preach? The Church's Urgent Question (David C. Norrington with Replies to the Critics & an Introduction by Jon Zens), 2013

- 58 to 0: How Christ Leads Through the One Anothers, 2013

WWW.JONZENS.COM

LOOKING FOR PAST ISSUES OF
SEARCHING TOGETHER?

A full set of back issues of Searching Together is available for $75 postpaid.

This set consists of over 90 published issues of our quarterly Journal from 1978 to 2018, many of which consist of multiple quarters.

These Journals contain many articles opening up aspects of our life in Christ, our life together in His body, and extending grace and forgiveness to one another.

You can order this set by either:

1. Sending a check for $75 to Searching Together, PO Box 548, St Croix Falls WI 54024

2. Visiting www.searchingtogether.org and donating $75 via PayPal by clicking on the "Donate" button.

You will be built up and challenged by reading these back issues spanning our 40+ year history!

SUBSCRIPTION INFO

SUBSCRIPTIONS

A subscription to *Searching Together* is available for $10 per year (United Kingdom £2 per issue). Discounts and free subscriptions are available to those who cannot afford the full subscription price. A discount of $7 per year is available for subscriptions involving five or more copies to the same address. A set of back issues from 1978 to present can be ordered from *Searching Together* for $75 postpaid. We will send a gift subscription to anyone from you for $5 per year.

INQUIRIES AND CORRESPONDENCE

If you want to reprint an article, please write to *Searching Together* for permission and include *Searching Together's* address in the credits. Articles may be reproduced for small-scale distribution without permission. Correspondence to authors should be sent to *Searching Together*.

CONTACT INFORMATION

United States
Searching Together/Jon Zens
P.O. Box 548
St. Croix Falls, WI 54024
jzens@searchingtogether.org
(715) 338-2796
www.searchingtogether.org

Australia
Ray Levick
Unit 25, 61-67 Moverly Rd
Maroubra 3035, Australia
rlevick77@gmail.com

Canada
Larry Hartley
2391 Route 114
Weldon, N.B.
Canada E4H 4R2
chegutu@nbnet.nb.ca

United Kingdom
Siobhan & Mike O'Leary
Beulah Print & Design
19 Fair Street
Drogheda Co, Louth, Ireland